SpringerBriefs in Law

For further volumes:
http://www.springer.com/series/10164

Carl Wellman

Terrorism and Counterterrorism

A Moral Assessment

Springer

Carl Wellman
Department of Philosophy
Washington University – St. Louis
St. Louis, MO
USA

ISSN 2192-855X ISSN 2192-8568 (electronic)
ISBN 978-94-007-6006-6 ISBN 978-94-007-6007-3 (eBook)
DOI 10.1007/978-94-007-6007-3
Springer Dordrecht Heidelberg New York London

Library of Congress Control Number: 2012954067

Printed on acid-free paper

Springer is part of Springer Science+Business Media (www.springer.com)

Contents

Chapter 1
What is Terrorism?

Abstract For the moral assessment of terrorism and counterterrorism, one needs a real descriptive definition of terrorism to identify one's subject matter and avoid misunderstanding. It is a mistake to omit violence from one's definition both because this is entrenched in ordinary language and because this is a crucial wrong-making characteristic of terrorism. However, one need not limit terrorism to political violence because one can treat political terrorism as one species of terrorism more broadly defined. For moral purposes, one should define terrorism as the attempt to coerce an indirect target by means of terror produced by the use or threat of violence against a direct target. Although it is true that terrorism can have a wide variety of purposes, not all of them are essential to its nature. It prejudices one's moral judgment of terrorism if one defines it as an attack upon the innocent because this suggests that it should be judged simply in terms of just war theory rather than a wider range of relevant moral reasons. To limit terrorism to the systematic use of violence ignores the moral similarity to such acts as kidnapping.

My purpose in this book is to investigate the morality of terrorism and to reach some conclusions about whether it is ever justified as well as how we ought to respond to it. As one would expect of an analytic moral philosopher, I will begin by seeking a definition of terrorism. More specifically, I will formulate and explain a definition, the one that is most adequate for my purposes of moral evaluation, not the definition to be imposed upon all investigators whatever their purposes. If a national legislature intends to make terrorism a crime, it will need a very different sort of definition, one limited to those acts that are most harmful. And in any treaty intended to reduce terrorism, it must be defined so as to limit its scope to terrorist acts with an international dimension.

1.1 Proposed Definitions

There have been many previous attempts, some more useful than others, to define terrorism. When I first began to investigate the morality of terrorism, I defined it as "the use or attempted use of terror as a means of coercion" (Wellman 1979,

C. Wellman, *Terrorism and Counterterrorism*, SpringerBriefs in Law 9,
DOI: 10.1007/978-94-007-6007-3_1, © The Author(s) 2013

p. 250). I deliberately proposed a very broad definition in order to resist the assumption that its morality could be determined merely by applying the moral theory usually applied to war, violence or revolution. I then explained that:

> At the conceptual core of my definition stand a pair or concepts, terror and coercion. Terror is the essential means and coercion the essential end. When a gunman confronts his victim and demands "your money or your life," he is using, or attempting to use, the terror he inspires in his victim as a means of coercing him into handing over his wallet (Wellman 1979, p. 251).

But not everyone would see the gunman's threat as a genuine instance of terrorism. It seems very different from paradigmatic instances such as the devastating action of the IRA in its 1996 Manchester bombing or the act of a suicide bomber in Iraq. And no one has agreed with me that I engaged in terrorism when I threatened to flunk any student who handed in his or her paper after the due date (Wellman 1979, p. 252). Hence, most theorists have proposed more narrow definitions of terrorism.

The obvious way to limit the definition of terrorism would be to include two features of paradigm examples, violence and a political purpose, that I omitted. Thus, Per Bauhn defines terrorism as "the performance of violent acts, directed against one or more persons, intended by the performing agent to intimidate one or more persons and thereby to bring about one or more of the agent's political goals" (Bauhn 1989, p. 28). But although the threat of an single gunman seems very different from most acts of terrorism, the "protection racket" of the mafia by which it obtains periodic payments from targeted businesses seems to qualify as genuine terrorism even though its goal is financial rather than political. Similarly, the brutal attacks of Mexican drug cartels upon the police and their mass killings of civilians are taken to be examples of terrorism by the media and both the Mexican and United States governments.

Nevertheless, many limit their examinations of the morality of terrorism to political terrorism. For example, C. A. J. Coady defines terrorism as "the organized use of violence to attack non-combatants ('innocents' in a special sense) or their property for political purposes (Coady 2004b, p. 5). But Virginia Held questions his limitation of terrorism to attacks on non-combatants:

> If targeting civilians must be part of terrorism, then blowing up the Marine barracks in Lebanon in 1985 and killing hundreds of marines, and blasting a hole in the U. S. destroyer Cole and killing seventeen sailors in Yeman in October 2000 would not be instances of terrorism, and yet they are routinely offered as examples of terrorism (Held 2008, p. 17).

One could, of course, restrict one's investigation of the morality of terrorism to attacks upon the innocent, but this would render one's conclusions irrelevant to a wide variety of violent attacks of great practical importance and similar moral import.

In addition to controversy about the victims of terrorism, there is disagreement about its perpetrators. As one would expect, governments typically characterize terrorism as illegal or immoral violence directed against themselves and do not consider their own use of violence as terrorism. After reviewing the changing meanings of terrorism through history, Bruce Hoffman defines contemporary terrorism as "the deliberate creation and exploitation of fear through violence or the threat of violence in the pursuit of political change." And he makes it clear that violence to pursue political change is necessarily "perpetrated by a subnational group or non-state entity" (Hoffman 1999, p. 43). But the Oxford English Dictionary reports that the original meaning of "terrorism" was "Government by intimidation as directed and carried out by the party in power in France during the Revolution of 1789–94." And Jenny Teichman observes:

> State terrorism: quite apart from historical considerations, we have to acknowledge that governments often do things, both to their own people, and against enemies in peace and war, which share the features of the worst types of revolutionary terrorism. State terrorism is characterized by such actions as the kidnapping and assassination of political opponents of the government by the police or secret service or the army; imprisonment without trial; torture; massacres of racial or religious minorities or of certain social classes; incarceration of citizens in concentration camps; and generally speaking government by fear (Teichman 1989, pp. 509–510).

A more recent analogue of the French Reign of Terror is the rule of Augusto Pinochet in Chile from 1973 to 1990 during which more than 3,200 people were executed or disappeared and thousands more were detained or tortured. It seems to many that the moral issues raised by governmental actions of these sorts are essentially the same as those posed by revolutionary terrorism. However, this brief survey of proposed definitions of terrorism suggests that any proposed definition of terrorism will be controversial at best and question-begging at worst.

1.2 Why Define?

Is it sensible to make one more attempt to define terrorism when reputable scholars have advocated well over one hundred definitions, none of which has been accepted by more than a very few colleagues? Given the widespread treatment of terrorism in the public media, it might seem more reasonable to begin by assuming that we share a concept of terrorism and the ability to apply it prior to any conceptual analysis. As some say of art or beauty, "I cannot define it, but I know it when I see it." In fact, many authors begin merely by describing historically important examples of terrorism before going on to develop their theories of terrorism. Unfortunately, their colleagues often deny that some of these are genuine instances of terrorism. This shows that either there is no widely shared conception of terrorism or that any shared conception is so unclear and imprecise that it would be inadequate for theoretical purposes. If so, it will be impossible to define the established meaning of "terrorism" in any useful way. However, this does not rule out introducing a stipulative definition for theoretical purposes.

But could any stipulative definition capture what is essential to or most important about terrorism? George P. Fletcher points out that the concept of terrorism fulfills multiple functions (Fletcher 2006, p. 900). I agree that the word "terrorism" is used in many contexts and by speakers or writers with a wide variety of purposes. A president or prime minister may apply the word to any violent attack upon his or her state but insist that any violent retaliation is not terrorism. When debating terrorism in the United Nations General Assembly, delegates from the third world argue that violent actions of freedom fighters are not terrorism while those from the dominant nation states insist on condemning any such violence as terroristic. A lawyer will typically think of terrorism as an actual or potential crime, but moral philosopher will be concerned only with its moral status as immoral or morally justifiable. And lawyers will conceive of terrorism differently depending upon whether they are considering its status in national or international law. But this does not imply, as the title of Fletcher's article suggests, that the concept of terrorism is indefinable. The lesson one should learn from the multiple purposes of the language of terrorism is that there could be a number of different definitions of terrorism and that one should adopt a definition appropriate to his or her purposes because what is most important about terrorism depends upon one's purposes. Thus, for the purposes of moral theory, one ought to define terrorism in terms of its most important morally relevant properties.

Unfortunately, there is persistent disagreement about what these properties are. Virginia Held reports that the definition of terrorism is notoriously difficult because it is one of the most contested concepts (Held 2008, p. 16). And Robert Young refrains from offering a definition of terrorism because he does not wish to give the impression that his account is not contested (Young 2002, p. 22). This suggests that the concept of terrorism is an instance of what W. B. Gallie called an essentially contested concept. An essentially contested concept is a complex evaluative concept such that disagreement about its appropriate application cannot be resolved because there is no universally accepted measure of the relative importance of its various evaluative aspects (Gallie 1955–1956, pp. 167–198). Hence, any definition will inevitably be partisan and be useless for the purposes of any objective moral or political theory. This may or may not be true. All the concepts of moral theory are notoriously difficult to define in any universally acceptable way. But this does not make conceptual analysis in moral theory impossible or even useless because each of a variety of conceptual perspective may be morally illuminating.

Nevertheless, one may well wonder whether defining terrorism is either necessary or useful for the purposes of moral theory. One source of disagreement and confusion concerning the morality of terrorism, although by no means the most important source, is that different individuals, especially those with diverse cultural backgrounds or trained in different disciplines, conceive of terrorism very differently. Therefore, anyone who wishes to explain to others one's views of the morality of terrorism and of national or international counter-measures, must define his or her conception of terrorism to avoid misunderstanding. As C. A. J. Coady reminds us:

> The point is that various issues about the rights and wrongs of terrorist acts, and, for that matter, anti-terrorist responses, cannot be addressed unless we are clear about what topic we are discussing. Too many debates about terrorism are at cross-purposes because of radical confusions about precisely what is being discussed(Coady 2004a, p. 3).

This makes it necessary to define terrorism in order to make it clear to one's audience which acts are included in and which excluded from one's discussion.

A second reason for a moral philosopher to define terrorism is to enable him or her to select out of all those violent actions that might be thought by some-one or other to constitute terrorism a determinate class of acts to consider. It will do this by specifying the essential similarities that serve as criteria for classifying some act as an instance of terrorism. As Stapley notes, this is necessary to ensure consistent and valid conclusions (Stapley 2009, p. 15). Too often, especially in conceptually confused matters, philosophers and more generally the public reason from true, or at least plausible, premises to conclusions that do not follow from them because of equivocation in their language.

A third reason for a moral philosopher attempting to establish conclusions about terrorism and counter-terrorism to define terrorism is to enable him or her to generalize. One could, of course, ignore borderline or controversial instances, select a small sample of paradigm examples of terrorism but refrain from any generic definition, and investigate the moral problems they present. However, one would not then be able to know how far, if at all, one's conclusions apply to other past or future acts that seem to be terrorism also. Hence, one's conclusions about paradigm examples might provide data for moral theory, but would not themselves constitute or add anything to even relatively specific moral theory because theory requires general hypotheses based upon evidence.

Finally, a philosopher concerned with the morality of terrorism and counter-terrorism ought to define terrorism in order to make his or her conclusions applicable to future practice. Grant Wardlaw rightly insists that:

> The communication problem is of more than academic importance. It is one of the root causes of both the vacillations in policy which characterize the responses of most individual states to terrorism and of the complete failure of the international community to launch any effective multi-lateral initiatives to combat terrorism (Wardlaw 1989, p. 4).

Politicians, lawyers, moralists and laypersons constantly debate in general terms issues concerning terrorism. If one's conclusions are to be relevant to these ongoing debates and apply to legislation, administrative decisions of policy or plans for future contingencies, they must in the end generalize beyond any preliminary set of examples of terrorism. Hence, some general definition will be required for any account of the morality of terrorism and of counter-terrorism that could provide guidance for the decisions facing our nation, other nation states and the international community.

1.3 What Kind of Definition?

The Oxford English Dictionary defines the noun "definition" as "A precise statement of the nature, properties, scope, or essential qualities of a thing; an explanation of a concept etc.; a statement or formal explanation of the meaning of a word or phrase." Similarly, philosophers distinguish between a real, a conceptual and a nominal definition. I will not attempt to define the meaning of the word "terrorism."

It is both vague and ambiguous in ordinary language and in the scholarly literature so that any nominal definition would be useless for constructing even a moderately clear and precise account of the morality of terrorism. Nor will I pretend to describe our concept of terrorism, for different individuals conceive of terrorism very differently. This is why one needs a definition if one is to avoid misunderstanding when one discusses the moral issues raised by terrorism or counter-terrorism. I will propose a real definition, one that specifies the essential characteristics of the class of terrorist actions that I will consider. This requires me to select as essential characteristics those that will best enable me to understand the moral problems terrorism poses and that will point to the considerations relevant to its moral evaluation.

I will propose a descriptive rather than a normative definition. The OED defines "normative" as "Establishing a norm or standard; of, derived from, or implying a standard or norm; prescriptive." Hence, any normative definition of terrorism would beg the question of its morality. For example, James M. Poland defines it as "the premeditated, deliberate, systematic murder, mayhem and threatening of the innocent to create fear and intimidation in order to gain a political or tactical advantage, usually to influence an audience." And Brian Jenkins writes: "Terrorism constitutes the illegitimate use of force to achieve a political objective when innocent people are targeted" (quoted in Coady 2002, p. 8). Any normative definition like these begs the question of whether terrorism is by its very nature always morally wrong. They prejudice, in the literal sense of judging in advance of rational inquiry, the answer to one of the central moral problems concerning terrorism, whether terrorism could under special circumstances be morally justified. Therefore, I will propose a descriptive definition, one that specifies the factual features by which I identify acts of terrorism. This is not to say that my definition will be morally neutral. Although the essential properties of acts of terrorism, such as violent and coercive, are not in themselves prescriptive, they are morally relevant factual characteristics that are, in the terminology of W. D. Ross, wrong-making, that is, characteristics that make an act wrong unless outweighed by one or more right-making characteristics. This leaves open the question as to whether the wrong-making properties of terrorism are ever outweighed by right-making properties. On the other hand, were one to define terrorism in such a manner as to render it innocuous, one would render mysterious the grave public concern it engenders and the urgent need for any philosophical investigation of its moral status.

More generally, I will propose as unprejudiced a definition as possible. There are many controversial moral questions that one ought to leave open when one defines terrorism. Among these are the following: Under what circumstances, if at all, could terrorism be justified? Do nation states ever engage in terrorism? What moral theory or set of theories best apply to terrorism and counter-terrorism? Does terrorism ever constitute an extreme emergency that justifies responses with no moral limits? Is the concept of terrorism applicable to freedom fighters? Do military tactics intended to break the morale of the enemy in a war ever constitute terrorism? Thus, one's definition of terrorism ought to leave room for reasoned argument to resolve a wide variety of moral issues.

1.4 A Revised Definition

When I first began investigating terrorism, almost three decades ago, I discovered that each of the authors most often cited focused on only one species of terrorism and judged it from a very narrow moral perspective.

> Most philosophical discussions of terrorism treat it as a species of warfare or of violence or of revolutionary action. Hence, the complex issues concerning the morality of terrorism are decided simply by applying one of the accepted moral justifications or condemnations of war, violence or revolution. But to approach the subject in this way is to prejudice, in the literal sense of implicitly prejudging, the manifold and urgent moral issues posed by the terrible presence of terrorism in our world today. Again, it is to ignore what is distinctive about terrorism as such (Wellman 1979, p. 250).

To avoid any such prejudice, I defined terrorism very broadly as "the use or attempted use of terror as a means of coercion" (Wellman 1979, p. 250).

In retrospect, I believe that it was a mistake to omit any reference to violence in my original definition in order to broaden the range of morally relevant considerations. I then explained:

> But the ethics of terrorism is not a mere footnote to the ethics of violence because violence is not essential to terrorism and, in fact, most acts of terrorism are nonviolent. The judge sentencing a condemned criminal to death is engaging in terrorism if he is deterring or attempting to deter potential criminals by using the terror of death innate in human nature. Blackmail, in which the fear of dreaded exposure is used as a means of intimidation, is another nonviolent form of terrorism. I must confess that I often engage in nonviolent terrorism myself, for I often threaten to flunk any student who hands in his paper after the due date (Wellman 1979, pp. 251–252).

Igor Primoratz has rightly criticized this passage:

> I agree that the ethics of terrorism is more than a footnote to the ethics of violence, but not for the reason adduced by Wellman. It seems to me that it would not make much sense to speak of 'non-violent terrorism' (in the sense which also excludes threats of violence). Wellman has three counter-examples, none of which strikes me as convincing (Primoratz 2004, p. 16).

Although one could intelligibly speak of non-violent terrorism, as I did, to do so is to deviate markedly from standard usage. Alex P. Schmid et. al. examined one hundred and nine definitions of terrorism and found that 83.5 % of them refer to violence or force, by far the most frequent definitional element (Schmid et al. 1988, pp. 5–6).

I probably imagined that many acts of terrorism are nonviolent because I was thinking of violence as "force or strength of physical action or natural agents; forcible, powerful, or violent action or motion ..." (Wellman 1991, pp. 170–171). On this conception of violence, the execution of a condemned criminal by lethal injection administered gently is nonviolent as are acts of mailing anthrax to public officials or stealthily poisoning the water supply of a city. However, a more relevant sense of violence is "...treatment or usage tending to cause bodily injury or forcibly interfering with personal freedom."

Interpreting violence in this sense, I would now redefine terrorism as "the attempt to coerce an indirect target by means of terror produced by the use or threat of violence against a direct target." In addition to limiting terrorism to actions that use or threaten violence, I now make explicit the distinction between direct and indirect targets only implicit in my previous definition. In the 9/11 attack on the World Trade Center, for example, the direct targets were the twin towers and the people working in them, while the indirect targets were the United States Government and more widely the American public supporting what Al Qaeda regarded as its unjust policies.

On my revised definition, the action of a gunman who threatens violence should the victim not hand over her purse would not constitute terrorism because there is no distinction between direct and indirect targets. However, kidnapping would be terrorism because the person kidnapped and those being coerced into paying ransom are distinct. This seems appropriate because hostage taking is a paradigm case of terrorism.

Again, capital punishment, at least when used as a deterrent, would be terrorism because it is an attempt to coerce an indirect target, potential criminals, by means of the execution of a convicted criminal, the direct target of violence. However, the threat of execution implicit in legislation prohibiting capital crimes would not be terrorism because the potential criminals threatened with violent death are the same as those the law is attempting to deter. Reflection on kidnapping, capital punishment and other borderline cases may well be illuminating because they are morally problematic for much the same reasons as paradigm instances of terrorism.

When identifying what might make capital punishment morally problematic, one must distinguish between the execution of a condemned criminal as punishment for his own past wrongdoing and his execution as a means of deterring others who might be tempted to engage in criminal activity in the future. As punishment, what is relevant is whether the condemned criminal is treated as he or she deserves, colloquially whether the punishment fits the crime. But as deterrence, capital punishment is judged, not by what the victim deserves but by its effectiveness, by whether the moral harms to potential victims outweighs the moral harm imposed upon the executed criminal. Regarded as a deterrent, an innocent person is just as good as a guilty one, provided that the public believes that he or she is being punished as a criminal. Hence, when executed to deter potential wrongdoers the condemned criminal is treated merely as a means and not respected as a moral agent capable of rational choice.

On my revised definition, terrorism has four essential features. There must be some act or set of acts that are or are intended to be terrifying. The resulting terror must be the dread of some very unacceptable consequence should the person or persons the terrorist is trying to coerce fail or refuse to act as demanded. This implies that every act of terrorism must be a threat that some great harm will be inflicted if the coercion is resisted. Finally, terrorism presupposes the distinction between the direct and the indirect target of violence, between the person(s) or property that suffers violence or the threat of violence and the person(s) the terrorist intends to coerce.

1.5 Plausible Objections

The most serious objection to my revised definition is that it fails to recognize that terrorist action can have several purposes other than coercion. Although several authors have described one or more of these purposes, the most systematic discussion of the non-coercive uses of terror is by Jeremy Waldron who writes:

> The characterization of people as terrorists is best understood as a characterization in terms of the means they use. I think it would be a mistake to try to define terrorists in terms of their characteristic ends, because these ends are many and varied and they are often capable (at least in principle) of being pursued by using non-terroristic means (Waldron 2010, p. 68).

I agree that one ought not to define terrorists by their ends or goals because they typically have a many goals and often pursue them by both terrorism and other means. I also agree that one ought to characterize terrorists by the means they use. Terrorists are people who use terrorism as a means to achieve their ends, whatever these ends may be. However, this leaves open the best definition of terrorism.

Still, it might be a mistake to define terrorism as an essentially coercive means. Waldron suggests that coercion has a typical structure:

(i) the coercer gets the victim in his power so that he can communicate the threat and impose the threatened harm if he has to; and
(ii) the coercer demonstrates the threat by actually imposing harms of the kind that he is threatening; and
(iii) the coercer by making the threat affects the decision-making of the victim; or
(iv) if the victim defies him, the coercer actually inflicts the harm (Waldron 2010, p. 54).

He then sums up his conclusion as follows:

> On the one hand, I wanted to argue that the strategies associated with terrorist action are not necessarily coercive; that they do not necessarily have the structure of demand-plus-threat. Some instances do have this structure; but in other cases the use of terrorist violence is associated with military or retributive or publicity-seeking or expressive or ethical strategies or strategies simply designed to discredit the targeted state (Waldron 2010, p. 78).

Granted that the strategies associated with terrorist action are not necessarily coercive, not everything associated with terrorism is definitive of it.

How does Waldron reason from his analysis of the structure of coercion to his conclusion that the strategies associated with terrorist action need not be coercive? The crucial step in his argument is this:

> But now I want to consider the possibility that element (ii) which is characteristic of terrorism, need not be part of a coercive strategy at all. What else might it be? A number of possibilities suggest themselves, each of which suggests a non-coercive model of terrorist action (in the simple demand-plus-threat sense of coercion) (Waldron 2010, p. 69).

He then describes seven such possibilities. Notice, however that element (ii) concerns violence, "imposing harms of the kind he is threatening," and that any terror that "affects the decision-making of the victim" belongs in element (iii).

Thus, the possibilities Waldron describes are primarily uses of violence, not necessarily uses of terror. The conclusion one ought to draw from this is that one needs to distinguish between the use of violence as a means to terror and those uses of violence with other ends. The possible uses of any terror produced by violence remain to be identified.

It is probably true that, as Waldron suggests, there are a variety of non-coercive uses of terror. However, I believe that one should distinguish between acts of violence as a means of producing terror within the context of a coercive endeavor and those that are not part of a coercive strategy. I would classify the former as acts of terrorism in which these uses of terror are intermediate ends that are in turn means of coercion. The latter are not acts of terrorism as I conceive of it. For example, violent acts of punishing an opponent that are intended to create dread of further punishment in order to coerce one's potential targets are instances of terrorism. But acts "intended as punishment or retaliation for some real or imagined offense, and not calculated to achieve anything beyond that" (Waldron 2010, p. 69) are not. Punishment as retribution with no further end is simply punishing by imposing harm; if it also creates terror or dread, that result is incidental. Similarly, an act "intended simply to attract publicity to the cause of those who perpetrate an atrocity, without any ulterior coercive intent" (Waldron 2010, p. 70) is not terrorism as I define it. But a similar act that is intended to attract publicity for one's cause in order to increase support for one's coercive strategy is terrorism.

Granted that one should distinguish between the uses of terror within a coercive context and outside of any such context, why should this distinction be definitive of terrorism? The primary reason is that paradigmatic acts of terrorism are coercive and that this is one of the facts that makes them morally problematic. Hence, for my purposes of moral assessment, essentially similar actions are those that are morally problematic for the same reasons. A secondary consideration is that uses of terror taken out of a coercive context are atypical, sporadic and present a less urgent threat. Hence, any serious and detailed consideration of their moral status can best be postponed until after one has examined the morality of terrorism of the paradigmatic kinds.

In the survey by Alex P Schmid and others of the definitional elements in one hundred and nine definitions of "terrorism," "political" ranked second with a frequency of 65 % (Schmid et al. 1988, pp. 5–6). Presumably many authorities on terrorism would object that my definition is too broad because it ignores the fact that terrorism is essentially political in nature. And there is a practical wisdom in those authors who limit their consideration of terrorism to political terrorism because it constitutes the most urgent threat to nation states, the international community and to large numbers of innocent victims due to its large scale and widespread effects.

Nevertheless, I believe that it would be a mistake for me to revise my definition to include the qualification that terrorism must be political in nature. What would I lose were I to revise my broad definition of terrorism and limit my conception to political terrorism? I would lose the illumination one can obtain by comparing and contrasting political terrorism with a wide variety of other kinds of action that are morally problematic for much the same reasons. And I would gain very little by revising my broad definition in this manner because one can examine political terrorism as one species of terrorism defined generically. Moreover, my broad definition already points to the most important features that render political terrorism morally problematic. However, there is a lesson to be learned from this objection. If one adopts a very broad definition of terrorism, one should supplement it with a classification of the most important species that fall under this conception. Only in this way can one compare and contrast various kinds of terrorism in a way that will be illuminating.

A third serious objection to my revised definition is that it fails to include one of the most important features that makes terrorism morally problematic, that terrorism attacks innocent victims. C. A. J. Coady defines terrorism as: "the organized use of violence to attack non-combatants ('innocents' in a special sense) or their property for political purposes" (Coady 2004a, p. 5). He notes that defining terrorism in terms of non-combatants:

> catches a central logical and moral aspect of common discourse employing the term since terrorism is frequently objected to because 'the innocent' are attacked. Indeed, this is probably the most common public complaint against terrorism, even if there remain many unclarities and even evasions about who are to count as innocent (Coady 2004a, p. 5).

It is true that terrorist acts are often vigorously condemned on this ground. But to build this wrong-making feature of those terrorist actions central to public debate into the definition of terrorism is to prejudice our moral evaluation by disregarding other morally relevant considerations.

In addition, Coady argues that:

> This approach also gives a handle for serious ethical discussion by linking terrorism to moral argument about wear, in particular (although not exclusively) to the just war tradition which imposes strong conditions for non-combatant immunity from direct attack (Coady 2004a, p. 5)).

Igor Primoratz similarly defines terrorism in terms of the use or threat of violence against innocent people and suggests that this definition "helps place the debate about the morality of terrorism in the context of the traditional discussion of the morality of war, and in particular connects it with just war theory" (Primoratz 2004, pp. 24–25).

I believe that it is a mistake to connect terrorism with just war theory by definition. This is not to deny that large-scale terrorism is analogous to warfare in many ways so that a consideration of just war theory may be morally illuminating. But some terrorist actions, such as the Oklahoma City bombing, are too isolated to qualify as acts of any war. Hence, it is unhelpful to place the debate about the morality of terrorism within the context of the morality of war. And it is a disadvantage to tie one's conception of terrorism to just war theory because this is only one of many moral theories that may well be applicable to acts of terrorism. One should not prejudice one's approach to the morality of terrorism by excluding a wide variety of potentially relevant moral perspectives.

Moreover, any application of a definition of terrorism in terms of noncombatants or the innocent will itself be morally problematic. Coady admits that:

> A difficulty with this definitional approach is that the concept of noncombatant needs clarification. Its moral significance also needs to be established against certain natural objections (Coady 2001, p. 1697).

Coady undertakes this project in his controversial article "Terrorism and Innocence" (Coady 2004a, pp. 37–58). The difficulty is not merely that there are a number of competing theories that attempt to distinguish between morally legitimate and illegitimate targets of violence. It is that in debates about terrorism any assertion that some use or threatened use of violence is terrorism could be dismissed by asserting that the victims are oppressors or persons who aid and abet the gross injustice against which the violence is aimed.

Also, and most crucially, any definition of terrorism in terms of the innocence of its victims will exclude several systematic uses of violence that are essentially similar to paradigmatic examples of terrorism in that they are morally problematic for much the same reasons. Thus, Michael Walzer, who describes terrorism as the random murder of innocent people, gives three examples of "so-called terrorists" who refrained or tried to refrain from targeting the innocent. These are the Russian revolutionaries who decided to assassinate the Grand Duke Sergei, the Irish Republican Army, and the Stern Gang, all of whom figure prominently in most historical surveys of terrorism (Walzer 1977, pp. 198–199). And Coady quoted the Cypriot revolutionary General George Grivas as reporting: "We did not strike, like the bomber, at random. We shot only British servicemen who would have killed us if they could have fired first, and civilians who were traitors or intelligence agents" (Coady 1985, p. 62).

More recently Stephen Nathanson has insisted upon including the innocence of the targets in defining terrorism.

Definition: Terrorist acts:

1. are acts of serious, deliberate violence or credible threats of such acts;
2. are committed in order to promote a political or social agenda;
3. generally target limited numbers of people but aim to influence a larger group and/or the leaders who make decisions for this group;
4. intentionally kill or injure innocent people or pose a threat of serious harm to them (Nathanson 2010, p. 24).

After explaining how this definition enables us to avoid many of the problems that have made defining terrorism difficult, he argues that a virtue of this definition is that it allows us to explain how terrorism is morally wrong.

Nathanson suggests that none of the first three conditions in his definition of terrorism can adequately explain the wrongness of terrorism because none of them implies that terrorism is necessarily wrong, that it is never morally justified whatever the circumstances. The heart of the matter is "the idea that terrorist acts *intentionally kill or injure innocent people or pose a serious threat of such harms to innocent people*" (Nathanson 2010, p. 33). Similarly, "According to condition 4, however, terrorism always and necessarily picks out innocent people to be its targets. This is what makes it plausible to believe that terrorism is always wrong" (Nathanson 2010, P. 34).

I agree that it is plausible to believe that terrorism is always wrong. Nevertheless, this is far from self-evident, and there are reputable moral philosophers who believe that although terrorism is almost always wrong, it might be morally justified in very exceptional circumstances. Therefore, I ought not to begin my investigation of the morality of terrorism and counter-terrorism by defining terrorism in a manner suggesting this conclusion.

More often Nathanson defends his definition of terrorism by suggesting that it explains how terrorism is especially or very seriously wrong. The innocence of the victims "seems to provide a plausible basis for understanding both why terrorist acts are wrong and why people condemn terrorism with special vehemence. It does this because there seems to be something especially terrible about targeting innocent people" (Nathanson 2010, p. 33). And "I do, however, defend the idea that there is something especially wrong about terrorism and that this special wrongness is related to the nature of its victims" (Nathanson 2010, p. 36).

Granted that there is something especially wrong about typical acts of terrorism, one need not appeal to the innocence of its victims to explain this. Nathanson includes the use or threat of serious violence in his definition of terrorism and recognizes that "Because acts of serious violence injure and kill their victims, commonsense morality generally condemns them" (Nathanson 2010, p. 310. I would add only that both the use and threat of violence harm their victims and violate human rights such as the rights to life, personal security and liberty. Moreover, condition 3 in Nathanson's definition is that terrorist acts "generally target limited numbers of people but aim to influence a larger group and/or the leaders who make decisions for the group" (Nathanson 2010, p. 24). In other words, they use limited numbers of people merely as a means to influence a larger group of people, a paradigmatic sort of immoral conduct. Finally my proposed definition of terrorism suggests that what Nathanson gently refers to as "the communicative aspect of terrorism" used to "influence others" (Nathanson 2010, p. 26) is more properly seen as an attempt to coerce the larger group of persons, and as coercive something that is seriously immoral. Hence, I will retain my broader definition that does not limit terrorism to the use or threat of violence against the innocent.

A fourth plausible objection to my revised definition is that it fails to recognize that terrorism is essentially systematic. Michael Bauer explains why this must be the case:

> Thus a petty thief who achieves his goal immediately and directly by robbing people—even if such acts of robbery are indiscriminate and random—is an ordinary criminal and not a terrorist. By contrast, a local gang leader is acting as a terrorist if he achieves his aim (e.g., preventing people from reporting to the police) by intimidating inhabitants in an entire neighborhood through a systematic policy of randomized violence. We can say, paradoxically, that terrorism involves the "systematically random" or "systematically unsystematic" use of violence for the purpose of creating and exploiting a climate of fear in certain sectors of society or in society as a whole (Bauer 2005, p. 14).

Thus it seems that although isolated threats of violence are often coercive, only a threat of widespread violence made credible by a system of violent acts can create the climate of fear needed by the terrorist.

> Similarly Uwe Steinhoff argues that terrorism involves a systematic strategy as follows:Would we speak of terrorism in the case of a kidnapping when other people, for example the relatives of the kidnapped person, are being blackmailed to pay ransom? Obviously not. So there is something missing....Thus, terrorism is the credible threat of repeated attacks on innocents. This does not exclude the possibility of one-off acts of terrorism: one violent act, without follow-ups, can still make a threat of *repeated* violent acts credible. However, a one-off act of violence can be called terrorist only if it is part of such a strategy that threatens more than one act of violence. Incidentally, this also corresponds to the origin of the words "terrorism" and "terror" in the French "*régime de la terreur*", the rule of terror of the Jacobins after the French Revolution (Steinhoff 2007, pp. 120–121).

Accordingly, he concludes that an act of violence can be a terrorist act only if it is an element in a larger system of actual or threatened actions.

I must admit that we would not speak of the actions of a kidnapper as terrorism in everyday conversation and that because my revised definition would apply to them it does go beyond ordinary language. Thus, the unabridged *Oxford English Dictionary* describes original uses of "terrorism" as references to "the system of the 'Terror' (1793–4)." And the *Mirriam-Webster Online Dictionary* defines "terrorism" as "the systematic use of *terror* especially as a means of coercion." However, this is not a conclusive objection because I am not pretending to report our everyday use of the word "terrorism" and its cognates. For the purposes of moral theory, one needs to define one's subject in a more clear and precise manner.

One could, of course, include systematicity in one's stipulative definition of terrorism, but I will not do so. For one thing, the term "systematic" would be misleading. A system consists of a whole made up of ordered parts. Hence, to define terrorism as systematic would suggest that only a series of actions could constitute terrorism. But even Steinhoff admits that a single violent act could be an instance of terrorism if it threatens one or more additional acts of violence. And my revised definition recognizes this because any infliction of violence could be coercive only if it threatens future violence. For another, it is unnecessary for the moral assessment of terrorism to require that it be systematic because systematicity does not introduce any new wrong-making characteristics. When a campaign of terrorism consists of a series of acts of violence, this fact is an aggravating factor because it multiplies the wrong-making characteristics of the individual violent action.

Finally, some will object that even though my revised definition is less broad than my original definition of terrorism, it is still too broad because it applies to acts that seem to be essentially different from paradigmatic terrorist acts. Let us examine the most plausible counter-examples.

(1) A kidnapping where the kidnapper is threatening harm to the victim in the event that relatives will not pay the demanded amount of money would constitute terrorism on my revised definition. But Uwe Steinhoff poses what he takes to be a rhetorical question: "Would we speak of terrorism in the case of a kidnapping when other people, for example the relatives of the kidnapped person, are being blackmailed to pay ransom? Obviously not." But why not? Steinhoff suggests that this is an isolated act and not systematic (Steinhoff 2007, p. 120). But I have argued that systematicity is not an essential feature

of terrorism. Others object to classifying kidnapping as terrorism because its purpose is personal profit rather than furthering any political or ideological cause. However, I have also argued that for the purposes of moral assessment, one should consider political terrorism only one species of a more general phenomenon. Doing so is doubly illuminating. It reminds one that kidnapping has the same wrong-making characteristics as paradigm examples of terrorism and that acts of terrorism may vary from being extraordinarily wrong to genuine but more ordinary wrongs.

(2) On my definition damage or destruction of property as a means of coercion would constitute terrorism. An apt illustration is a passage from *Newsweek* of January 7, 1985.

> Last June the Ladies Center, the only abortion clinic in Pensacola, Fla., was demolished by a still unsolved predawn bombing. At 3:23 on Christmas morning, vigilantes struck again, detonating a bomb in the new Ladies Center offices near Pensacola Regional Airport. Within 22 min, bombs also exploded in the offices of two local gynecologists who perform abortions. Although no one was injured in the blasts, the offices of Dr. William Perlmenter were gutted by fire and the three explosions did an estimated $375,000 in damage. Perlmenter later said he would no longer perform in-office abortions and complained that no one would rent to him because of the insurance risk. Dr. Bo Bagenholm, declared, "This isn't going to stop anything."

Jenny Teichman would refuse to consider these acts as genuine terrorism because no one was injured in the blasts.

> Destruction of property is not terrorism unless it is a precursor of a different kind of action i. e., part of a campaign which includes physically harming human beings. Thus the destruction of property by the suffragettes ought not to count as terrorism, whereas the destruction of glass on Kristallnacht certainly was, because of the attacks on Jews which followed (Teichman 1989, p. 512).

But if destruction of property in order to create coercive terror is not in itself terrorism, why would its association with other actions of physically harming human beings make any essential difference? After all, to damage property is to harm people, those human beings who own the property and depend upon it for their welfare. Elsewhere Teichman explains that the destruction of property in itself is not terrorism because it is not likely to produce terror—only fury (quoted in Primoratz 2004, p. 21). However, this is to misunderstand the sense in which terror is a means of coercion. What is intended is to create dread of fearful consequences, not necessarily any extreme agitation in the targeted persons.

(3) At first glance, the most implausible implication of my revised definition of terrorism is that it would recognize the use of harsh punishments, such as the death penalty, to deter potential criminals as terrorism. Some would object that the state has a right to use violent means to maintain law and order. Others would argue that harsh punishment, perhaps even capital punishment, is justified as retribution for the wrong done and to prevent the condemned person from further acts of crime. But these objections are beside the point. I am not denying that the state has a right, within limits, to use violent means of law-enforcement or asserting that even harsh punishment for retribution is terrorism.

Only when harsh punishment is used to instill fear into potential criminals and thus coerce them into obeying the law is it essentially similar to other acts of terrorism. One is tempted to deny this because deterrence, even harsh deterrence for serious crimes, seems morally justified, unlike paradigmatic acts of terrorism that strike us as grossly immoral. But a virtue of my broad definition of terrorism is that it does not imply that terrorism is necessarily immoral whatever the circumstances. That question remains open for reasoned discussion.

1.6 Conclusion

My goal is to investigate the morality of terrorism and to reach some conclusions about why it is normally wrong, whether it is ever justified and how we ought to respond to it. Given the facts that there is no clear and unambiguous meaning of "terrorism" established in ordinary language and that theorists have proposed over one hundred different definitions of terrorism, I need to define terrorism in order to select my subject matter and to prevent my readers from misunderstanding what I write. In this chapter I explain and defend a broad descriptive real definition. I propose a broad definition because I do not wish to limit in advance the kind of moral theory or theories that are relevant to my subject. I give a descriptive rather than a normative definition so as not to beg the question of whether terrorism can ever be morally justified. And I advocate a real rather than a lexical definition because my goal is to assess the morality of acts of terrorism, not merely to elucidate the meaning of words like "terrorism" and "terrorist."

Decades ago I defined terrorism as "the use or attempted use of terror as a means of coercion." Igor Primoratz and others have criticized my original definition because it implies that terrorism can be nonviolent. In retrospect, I believe that their objection is sound. Therefore, I now adopt a revised definition of terrorism as "the attempt to coerce an indirect target by means of terror produced by the use or threat of violence against a direct target." However, I reject five other plausible objections to my revised definition: that terrorism has several defining purposes in addition to coercion, that terrorism is essentially political, that terrorism always attacks innocent victims, that terrorism is necessarily systematic, and that my revised definition is too broad because it applies to acts that are clearly not instances of terrorism.

References

Bauer M (2005) In: Shanahan T (ed) Philosophy 9/11: thinking about the war on terrorism. Open Court, Chicago, pp 3–21

Bauhn Per (1989) Ethical aspects of political terrorism: the sacrificing of the innocent. Lund University Press, Lund

Coady CAJ (1985) The morality of terrorism. Philosophy 60:47–69
Coady C AJ (2001) Terrorism. In: Becker LC, Becker CB (eds) Encyclopedia of ethics, 2nd edn. Routledge, New York
Coady CAJ (2002) In: Coady T, O'Keefe M (eds) Terrorism and justice: moral argument in a threatened world. Melbourne University Press, Carlton
Coady CAJ (2004a) Terrorism and innocence. J Ethics 8:37–58
Coady CAJ (2004b) Defining terrorism. In: Primoratz I (ed) Terrorism: The Philosophical Issues. Palgrave Macmillan, Houndsville
Fletcher GP (2006) The indefinable concept of terrorism. J Int Crim Justice 4:894–911
Gallie WB (1955–1956) Essentially contested concepts. Proc Aristot Soc 56:167–198
Held Virginia (2008) How terrorism is wrong: morality and political violence. Oxford University Press, Oxford
Hoffman B (1999) Inside terrorism. Inigo, London
Nathanson S (2010) Terrorism and the ethics of war. Cambridge University Press, Cambridge
Primoratz I (2004) What is terrorism? In: Primoratz I (ed)Terrorism: the philosophical issues. Palgrave Mcmillan, Houndsvill
Schmid AP, Jongman AJ, Horowitz IL (1988) Political terrorism: a new guide to actors, authors, concepts, data bases, theories and literature. Transaction Books, New Brunswick
Stapley C (2009) Terrorism: its goals, targets, and strategies. In: Lowther AB, Lindsay B (eds) Terrorism's unanswered questions. Proeger Security International, Westport, pp 15–31
Steinhoff U (2007) On the ethics of war and terrorism. Oxford University Press, Oxford
Teichman J (1989) How to define terrorism. Philosophy 64:505–517
Waldron J (2010) Torture, terror, and trade-offs: philosophy for the white house. Oxford University Press, Oxford
Walzer M (1977) Just and unjust wars. Basic Books, New York
Wardlaw G (1989) Political terrorism: theory, tactics, and counter-measures, 2nd edn. Cambridge University Press, Cambridge
Wellman C (1979) On terrorism itself. J Value Inq 13:250–258
Wellman C (1991) Violence, law, and basic rights. In: Brady JB, Garver N (eds) Justice, law and violence. Temple University Press, Philadelphia, pp 170–186
Young R (2002) Political terrorism as a weapon of the politically powerless. In: Coady T, O'Keefe M (eds) Terrorism and justice: moral argument in a threatened world. Melbourne University Press, Carlton, pp 55–64

Chapter 2
Why is Terrorism Wrong?

Abstract Terrorism, as best defined, has four generic wrong-making characteristics. It uses or threatens violence. It typically produces terror. It uses persons as means without respecting them as autonomous moral agents. It attempts to coerce. These make terrorism morally wrong because they involve the infliction of serious harm and the violation of human rights. Political terrorism is also wrong because it undermines trust, generates conflict within a liberal society, undermines the capacity for self-government and disrupts social order. State terrorism violates the duty of nation states to protect citizens from harm and the violation of their human rights. International terrorism threatens peace and security and violates the sovereignty of nations. Racial terrorism always violates the moral right to equitable treatment of its victims and often oppresses members of the terrorized race. Family quasi-terrorism violates one's special moral responsibilities to members of one's family, destroys the necessary conditions for intimacy and often causes post-traumatic stress disorder. None of these wrong-making characteristics is limited to innocent victims; innocence is primarily relevant because it excludes any justification of terrorism as a defense against wrongful aggression.

Terrorism has an unsavory reputation. Whether it is always morally wrong is controversial, but hardly anyone can deny that it is always prima facie wrong. Surely terrorism is morally wrong unless there is some justifying reason strong enough to outweigh the important moral considerations that normally make it grievously wrong. I have defined terrorism as the attempt to coerce an indirect target by means of terror produced by the use or threat of violence against a direct target. This definition points to four essential characteristics that individually and collectively explain why it is by its very nature morally wrong. It (1) attempts to coerce an indirect target (2) by means of terror (3) produced by the use or threat of violence against a direct target (4) who is thus used merely as a means of coercion. Let us begin by examining these generic wrong-making characteristics.

2.1 The Use or Threat of Violence

Terrorists often use violence against their primary targets. Violence consists in treatment or usage tending to cause bodily injury or forcibly interfering with personal freedom. The obvious reason that the use of violence is prima facie morally

DOI: 10.1007/978-94-007-6007-3_2,

wrong is that injury and interference with liberty harm the victims. Hare describes some of the harms that might be inflicted by a terrorist using violence.

> He is, say, killing a lot of people in an airport lounge with a sub-machine gun; he is bereaving their children and spouses (and bereavement is often the greatest of human ills); he is wounding others; he is disrupting air travel, which may have far-reaching though hard-to-measure consequences if people who ought to go to places decide not to for fear of such attacks; he is causing governments and airlines to spend a lot of money on precautions against terrorism, and so increasing taxes and the price of air travel; and so on (Hare 1979, p. 245).

Similarly, suicide bombing typically causes severe harm to primary targets, often collateral damage to property or nonhuman animals or both, and has harmful consequences for other individuals who may or may not be friends or relatives of the immediate victims of violence.

Trudy Govier explains convincingly why there is a presumption that the use of violence is morally wrong. She notices, as Hare does not, that in addition to causing grievous harms, violence violates fundamental moral rights.

> Fundamentally the basis of this presumption is that the entities damaged or destroyed in acts of physical violence have value in themselves or in virtue of their function and use. Persons are believed to have a right to life that should be overridden only when absolutely necessary. Animals have value as sentient creatures and as serving biological or other needs of persons….Any ethic in which persons, environment, and properties are deemed to possess positive value yields by implication the presumption that it is wrong to harm or destroy them. Thus a presumptive case against physical violence emerges logically from any ethic in which one grants rights to persons, presumptions against harm to sentient creatures, and value to the interests of human beings and other sentient creatures and their need for resources (Grovier 2005, p. 114).

Even when the use of violence does not kill its primary targets, it usually inflicts serious injury on them or damages their property. Hence, the use of violence is typically morally wrong because it causes very serious harms and violates human rights such as the rights to life, personal security and property. Here is the most obvious explanation of why terrorism is grossly immoral unless there is some justifying reason sufficient to outweigh these wrong-making considerations.

Terrorists often refrain from actually using violence and merely threaten to use it. What, for example, is wrong with high-jacking an airplane or taking a few hostages if they are later released "unharmed"? Although the hostages may not be physically harmed, they are still harmed in at least four ways. The threat of violence, especially being killed or injured, is experienced as distressing, even agonizing. This is a relatively minor harm, but a genuine harm nevertheless. The threat of being subjected to serious violence often causes the primary targets of terrorism to modify their lifestyles, perhaps by avoiding places or discontinuing activities they now consider dangerous, thereby making their lives less satisfying to themselves and less useful to others. Sometimes the threat so shocks its victims that it causes a trauma resulting in lasting psychological damage or even leading to neurosis. And any threat of violence tends to escalate to the use of violence thus imposing the risk of death or injury upon direct targets.

Even when no such escalation occurs, the threat of violence violates the human right to personal security. Because a person is as much or more a psychological entity as a physical body, the right to personal security is the right not to be subjected to either psychological or physical injury. Hence, being subjected to the experience of distress or agony and possible psychological trauma violates this basic human right. And because one's bodily integrity is not secure when one is subjected to the risk that the threat will escalate into the use of violence, one's human right to person security is violated in a second way. It may be that the threat of violence is a less serious moral wrong than the use of violence, but it is far from a minor wrong to its victims.

2.2 The Production of Terror

Terrorism usually does and is always intended to produce terror in its indirect targets. But this is typically not terror in the strict sense defined by the OED as "The state of being terrified or extremely frightened; intense fear or dread; an instance of this." It is terror in a broader sense of deep anxiety or fear. What defines this sort of terror is not the felt intensity of the emotion but the seriousness attributed to the feared harm. Why do indirect targets take the dangers of terrorism so seriously? Jan Narveson describes three characteristics of terrorism that might explain this feature of the sort of terror it produces.

> *Sense of risk*. First, for the affected public at large, there is the uncertainty of life it engenders: an increased probability of persons unknown visiting evils upon us without our being able to anticipate them.... *Powerlessness*. Secondly, these risks, no different in kind and considerably less in degree than those facing the frontline soldier in wartime, differ from the soldier's case not only in that we have no control over the fact of being put at those risks, but also in that we have no way of even knowing that we have assumed them... .*Apparent absurdity*. A further feature often adds to the agony of the phenomenon from the point of view of the ordinary person. This is what we might call the putative absurdity of terrorism as a method of achieving the terrorist's aims (Narveson 1991, pp. 124–125).

No doubt the incessant and graphic publicity given by the media to acts of terrorism also insinuates that they should be taken seriously.

Why might the production of terror be morally wrong? Fear and anxiety are disagreeable feelings that are intrinsically evil. And anxiety tends to be pervasive and thereby make one unable to fully enjoy what would otherwise be much more valuable experiences. More harmful is the way in which terror undermines one's practical rationality. There is considerable evidence that indirect targets typically overestimate the risks of terrorism. For example, the deaths and injuries caused by automobile accidents in Europe and the United States each year vastly outnumber those resulting from terrorism. Yet almost no one chooses to avoid driving while large numbers of persons cancelled or refrained from taking long-distance flights after 9/11. Terrorism produces an anxiety that makes indirect targets make unreasonable sacrifices in their own lives and too often motivates them to act in ways that reduce the value of their contributions to the lives of others. In these ways, and perhaps in others, the production of terror is prima facie morally wrong because it is harmful.

2.3 Using Persons

Terrorists use or threaten violence upon their direct targets in order to produce terror in their indirect targets. Thus, they are using the former as means to their end of terrorizing. In the case of political terrorism, they are typically using the terror produced to put pressure upon some political body to modify its policies. Hence, they are also using their indirect targets as means. As Scheffler observes:

> Using Kantian terminology, we might say that the primary victims are treated not just as means to an end but as means to a means: that is, they are treated as a means to the end of treating the secondary victims as means to an end. Those who engage in this kind of terrorism do not merely display callous indifference to the grief, fear and misery of the secondary victims; instead, they deliberately use violence to cultivate and prey on those reactions. This helps to explain why there is something distinctively repellent about terrorism, both morally and humanly (Scheffler 2006, pp. 9–10).

Kant did not, of course, believe that it is always wrong to treat people as means. There is nothing wrong with using a taxi driver to get where one wants to go or a doctor to restore one to good health as long as they freely choose to assist one in these ways. What is morally wrong is treating people as means only, treating people as means without at the same time treating them as ends in themselves (Kant 1949, p. 87).

But what is it to treat someone as an end in himself or herself? Kant suggests, but does not clearly explain, his answer to this question.

> Beings whose existence does not depend on our will but on nature, if they are not rational beings, have only a relative worth as means and are therefore called "things"; on the other hand, rational beings are designated "persons," because their nature indicates that they are ends in themselves, i.e., things that may not be used merely as a means. Such a being is thus an object of respect and, so far, restricts all [arbitrary] choice. Such beings are not merely subjective ends, whose existence as a result of our action has worth for us but are objective ends, i.e., beings whose existence in itself is an end. Such an end is one for which no other end can be substituted, to which these beings should serve merely as means (Kant 1949, pp. 86–87).

In sum, to treat persons as an ends in themselves is to respect their individuality and practical rationality, that is to limit one's treatment of them by deferring to their individual capacities to choose and act on the basis of practical reasons. This strikes me as a profound, but deeply puzzling, moral insight.

Why is it wrong to fail to respect the individuality and rationality of persons? Kant's answer is implicit in the following passage:

> The ends which a rational person arbitrarily proposes to himself as consequences of his action are material ends and are without exception only relative, for only their relation to a particular constituted faculty of desire in the subject gives them their worth....But suppose

> that there were something the existence of which in itself had absolute worth, something which, as an end in itself, could be the ground of definite laws. In it, and only in it, could lie the ground of a possible categorical imperative, i.e., of a practical law. Now, I say, man and, in general, every rational being exists as an end in himself and not merely as a means to be arbitrarily used by this or that will (Kant 1949, p. 86).

In other words, a person's capacity for rational choice and action makes him an end in himself with an absolute value, a value not relative to or derived from any subjective desire or inclination. And treating him as a means only would be contrary to his absolute value.

To my mind, this explanation raises several questions that Kant does not, and perhaps could not, answer persuasively.

(1) Why assume that a rational person selects his or her ends arbitrarily, for no valid reason? Kant asserts that our goals, the objects we strive to attain or achieve, have value merely because we desire them; but a more adequate theory of value would suggest that a rational agent desires this rather than that, because it is more desirable, because it has good-making characteristics that make it more valuable. Hence, Kant's distinction between objects with merely relative values and persons with an absolute value is dubious.

(2) How could the capacity for practical reason, as Kant conceives of it, give a person any value at all, much less an absolute value? Kant insists that practical reason must be pure, free of all desires or inclinations and, more generally, everything empirical (Kant 1949, p. 84). But to have value is to be desirable, satisfactory, admirable or, in the case of virtue, worthy of moral approval. Thus, the concept of value implies an emotional aspect excluded by Kant's conception of pure practical reason (Wellman 1961, pp. 207–227).

(3) Even if the capacity for practical reason did confer absolute value, how could this impose any moral obligation not to treat a person as a means only? I can understand how this might possibly imply an obligation not to perform a prefrontal lobotomy or to administer any drugs that would interfere with one's rational deliberation, for such acts would destroy or diminish one's capacity for practical reasoning and thereby reduce or eliminate one's absolute value. But most ways of treating someone as a means only, such as fraudulent advertising in order to sell defective products to unsuspecting customers or stealthy theft or forcible rape, leave the victim's capacity for practical reason intact and thus have no impact on his or her absolute value.

Why, then, is there any moral duty to respect the rational agency of others? As I explained some years ago:

> Rational agency involves setting one's goals, selecting ways of achieving them, and integrating ends and means into a more or less coherent life. But this becomes impossible, or at best very difficult, if others do not defer to one's decisions and yield to one's actions. It is projects that enable one to realize one's valued goals, and one's projects give the coherence and meaning to one's life that make it more than a series of trivial satisfactions. Hence, to disrespect the rational agency of another by interfering with her action is to reduce her control over her life and thereby to threaten what matters most to the value of her life (Wellman 2005, p. 44).

Clearly it would be morally wrong to inflict such a grievous harm upon any person. And because what is morally relevant about a person's rational agency is its importance for his or her own life, this requires one to respect the individuality of each and every person, to refrain from imposing one's own will against the will of another rational agent.

Terrorists typically treat their targets without sufficient concern for their individual capacities for rational choice. Sara Ruddick describes the intentions of the pilots who flew their planes into the World Trade Center.

> The pilots, if their Primer is to be trusted, also thought they were killing a kind—"the Unfaithful," "the Infidels." But the people who would become the victims on the planes and in the buildings are curiously absent from the reports about the pilots and from their preoccupied self-reflections in the primer. It is as if victims who were nothing but a "kind" became victims who were merely fungible accessories to a plan that inevitably involved the death of passengers and office workers whoever they might be. To paraphrase Simone Weil, in those planes, in those buildings, "they were nothing. They simply did not count" (Ruddick 2003, p. 216).

In other words, they were treated as mere means because the pilots treated them in ways to which no one of them could rationally consent.

Terrorists always use their direct targets as mere means by using or threatening violence upon them against their wills in order to produce terror in their indirect targets. And they often treat their indirect targets as mere means by inflicting terror upon them without their consent as a means of causing some political body to alter its policies. Therefore, terrorism is morally wrong unless there is some overriding justification for failing to respect the rationality of each of its individual targets.

2.4 An Attempt to Coerce

Terrorism, as I have defined it, is an attempt to coerce. Hence, if successful, it is prima facie wrong because coercion is harmful, and it is prima facie wrong to harm anyone. The one who is coerced is forced to act against her will. Thus, at the very least she will feel frustrated by not being able to act as she would have chosen. Given the diversity of human desires and lifestyles together with the special circumstances of our individual lives, each individual is normally the best judge of what is in her interest and the most motivated to act on her best judgment. Therefore, by forcing one to act against her best judgment, coercion will usually force one to sacrifice some portion of her welfare. And when a moral decision is involved, coercion is typically wrong because it denies a conscientious moral agent the opportunity to act in the morally right manner.

But suppose the attempt to coerce fails because the target evades or overcomes its force. It is still harmful for much the same reasons. Being forced to evade or resist attempted coercion is frustrating because it is being forced to act in some way one would not freely choose to act. And coerced evasive or resisting action equally denies one the opportunity to act on one's best prudential or moral judgment. However, when an attempt to coerce fails because the target is unaware of it or not threatened by it, then it is not harmful in any obvious way.

Nevertheless, any attempt to coerce normally does violate the moral right to liberty, a right with a broader scope than the right to liberty in most national legal systems. The defining core of this right is the moral liberty to act or refrain from acting in any way one chooses unless in so acting one would be violating a moral duty. The most relevant associated position in this right is the moral duty of all second parties not to prevent or hinder the right-holder from exercising her core moral liberty. Although one may sometimes be justified in infringing this very broad moral right to liberty, it is always prima facie wrong to deny its exercise to any normal human being. Hence, any attempt to coerce is almost always prima facie wrong because it is harmful to the person one coerces or attempts to coerce and always infringes her moral right to liberty.

The subject of my moral assessment is terrorism defined as the attempt to coerce an indirect target by means of terror produced by the use or threat of violence against a direct target. Thus defined, terrorism has four generic wrong-making characteristics—the use or threat of violence, the production of terror, using persons as means only, and the attempt to coerce. However, my very broad definition of terrorism ignores the differences between the various species of terrorism. Because the defining features of terrorism are not the only ones that explain why it is prima facie wrong, and may not even be the most serious ones, any adequate moral assessment must examine at least the most important species of this genus.

2.5 Political Terrorism

The most common and for the general public the paradigmatic kind of terrorism is political terrorism. Indeed, many authorities define terrorism in terms of its political motivation or goal. Several authors identify distinctive wrongs specific to political terrorism. For example, Michael Bauer argues that political terrorism undermines trust in a context of mutual dependence and puts a liberal society into conflict with itself.

> As systematically unsystematic violence, terrorism undermines trust on two levels: (a) it undermines the citizens' trust in the government's ability or will to protect them, and (b) it undermines the citizens' trust in one another as individuals. Terrorism thus has the effect of delegitimizing and destabilizing social institutions and relationships that are based on trust, and supplanting such institutions and relationships with ones that are based on fear or coercion (Bauer 2005, p. 20).

And the consequences for a liberal society are especially profound.

> Terrorism is a challenge to modern liberal societies not only "from the outside," but also "from the inside." This is because civil society's attempt at preserving itself through the "war on terrorism" requires the increasing surveillance of possibly innocent transactions, and the use of overwhelming force against the perceived perpetrators and sponsors of terrorism….Thus the more we execute the war on terror (a war we cannot fail to engage in some fashion), the more we run the risk of using means that are difficult to distinguish from those used by the terrorists themselves (Bauer 2005, p. 21).

To the extent that political terrorism is widespread and effective, it does have these consequences. And because they are very serious harms to a society and to its members, this makes political terrorism prima facie wrong.

Goodin describes a rather different way in which political terrorism harms a democratic society.

> People who are terrified do not reason clearly. They are panicked or cowed. Terrorism, insofar as it succeeds in producing terror, would thus have the effect of undermining people's capacity for autonomous self-government, both individually and collectively. Therein, I suggest, lies the distinctively *political* wrong of terrorism, understood as 'acts intended to frighten people for political advantage' (Goodin 2006, p. 158).

This diagnosis is confirmed by the tendency, even in nations with a strong democratic tradition, to uncritically accept pronouncements of its leaders and to confer upon its administration powers to curtail the constitutional rights of its citizens. To my mind, these are very serious political harms.

Scheffler argues that political terrorists take the insights of Thomas Hobbes to heart.

> In "the standard cases," terrorists undertake to kill or injure a more or less random group of civilians or noncombatants, in so doing, they aim to produce fear within some much larger group of people, and they hope that this fear will in turn erode or threaten to erode the quality or stability of an existing social order. I do not mean that they aim to reduce the social order to a Hobbesian state of nature, but only that they seek to degrade or destabilize it, or to provide a credible threat of its degradation or destabilization, by using fear to compromise the institutional structures and disrupt the patterns of social activity that help to sustain that order. The fear that terrorism produces may, for example, erode confidence in the government, depress the economy, distort the political process, reduce associational activity and provoke destructive changes in the legal system (Scheffler 2006, p. 5).

Although political terrorism is seldom if ever effective enough to produce all of these harmful consequences, it often has some such consequences. And to this extent, it is morally wrong. The special features of political terrorism identified by these authors add to its prima facie wrongness grounded on the generic nature of terrorism

2.6 State Terrorism

The subject of this section is state terrorism in the narrow sense defined as terrorism perpetrated by a nation state against members of its own population. Paradigm examples are the eighteenth century French Reign of Terror and the twentieth century Red Terror of the Bolshevik regime under Lenin. In this narrow sense, state terrorism does not include state-sponsored terrorism such as that of the Hizballah in Lebanon and Hamas in Palestine sponsored by Iran or the international terrorism that occurs when one state commits terrorism against the citizens of another state.

The distinctive wrong-making characteristics of state terrorism are implicit in Article 7 of the *Universal Declaration of Human Rights* that reads in part: "All are equal before the law and are entitled without any discrimination to equal protection of the law." State terrorism is morally wrong because it violates the moral responsibility of a nation state to protect its citizens from harm and the moral right of its citizens to equitable treatment.

Any nation state has a moral obligation to protect its citizens from harm. This is because by instituting and enforcing a legal system it prohibits its citizens, with very few exceptions, from using force against one another. Thus, it prevents or hinders the individuals over whom it has jurisdiction from almost all forms of self-help should their lives, bodies or property be wrongfully attacked. Therefore, simply by governing its population it invites, even requires, them to rely upon the state for protection from wrongful harm. If it subsequently commits acts of terrorism against its own citizens, it betrays the reasonable reliance it has invited, which is morally wrong. Indeed, not only does it fail to fulfill its moral duty to protect them from harm, it wrongfully harms them itself.

State terrorism is directed against "the enemy within," that portion of its citizens that the government believes, correctly or incorrectly, threaten its power to rule as it wishes. By terrorizing some members of its population while sparing others, it violates their moral right to equitable treatment, their right not to be treated worse than others similarly situated without a just-making reason (Wellman 1982, pp. 139–146). Accordingly, state terrorism is a very serious kind of immoral discrimination. However, when a state enforces its just laws, it does not violate the right to equitable treatment because the justice of its legal system constitutes a just-making reason for treating those who act illegally worse than those who obey the law. Accordingly, the specific wrong-making characteristics of state terrorism are that it violates the moral duty of a nation state to protect its population from harm and their moral right to equitable treatment under law.

2.7 International Terrorism

Terrorism is international when nationals of one state or quasi-state use or threaten violence, or aid and abet the use or threat of violence, against the persons or property subject to the jurisdiction of another state or quasi-state. Examples of quasi-states would be colonies of some governing nation state or territories such as Palestine that have extensive but limited authority of self-government but are not recognized as sovereign states in international law. Paradigm examples of international terrorism are terrorist acts of the IRA against persons or property in the United Kingdom, rocket fire or suicide bombing by members of the PLO or Hamas against Israelis, and most spectacularly the 9/11 bombing of the World Trade Center. The international dimension of this species of terrorism introduces additional distinctive wrong-making characteristics.

Although Leiser's definition of terrorism is unduly prejudicial, his analogy between international terrorism and piracy is illuminating.

> Pirates were regarded as enemies of mankind because they acknowledged no law, because they acted as if they were a law unto themselves....To be sure, the system of international law is still frail and rudimentary, but there is clearly *some* sense in which such a system does exist. In any event, it is the principal means adopted by the peoples of the world to assure peace among nations. One who flouts this fragile system, who transgresses against the sovereign rights of peoples and governments in their own territories or who violates the fundamental norms of international society, must stand condemned as an international outlaw and be regarded as if he had in fact declared war upon the system and upon all who owe allegiance to it and to the values it is designed to preserve (Leiser 1986, p. 409).

Here Leiser points to at least two wrong-making characteristics of international terrorism.

By violating international law in such a notorious manner, it threatens the peace and security of the international community. The primary purpose of international law is to preserve peace and promote friendly relations among the nations of the world. Although it is not entirely successful in this regard, it does contribute to these ends to a considerable extent. Because many terrorists disregard international law, including the Geneva Conventions, they undermine these norms and increase the possibility of international conflict or even warfare, declared or undeclared, between nations. International terrorism is prima facie wrong because it imposes the risk of these serious harms upon mankind. That this risk is both real and grave can be seen in the continuing conflicts in Afghanistan and Iraq.

Because international terrorism consists of the use or threat of violence by citizens of one state or quasi-state against persons or property in one or more other nation states, it violates the sovereignty or quasi-sovereignty of the invaded nations. Such attacks on national sovereignty are morally wrong, not only because sovereignty is a fundamental principle of international law, but also because of the moral justification of preserving state sovereignty. Both internal sovereignty, jurisdiction over all those residing in its territory, and external sovereignty, independence from coercion by outside forces, are necessary conditions for effective government. And effective government is necessary in order for state officials to protect their nationals from harm and to protect the human rights of their citizens. Therefore, any act that infringes national sovereignty, at least when it is exercised in a morally justified manner, tends to harm the inhabitants of a state and to reduce their exercise and enjoyment of their rights. In both regards, international terrorism is prima facie morally wrong.

2.8 Racial Terrorism

Racial terrorism is terrorism intended to terrorize the members of another race. Thus, what defines it as specifically racial is the racial identity of its indirect targets, not that of its direct targets. Although it inflicts violence or the threat of violence primarily upon members of another race, it also targets same-race individuals who support or are thought to sympathize with the race it is designed to terrorize. A paradigm example of racial terrorism is the activities of the Ku Klux Klan after the Civil War freed the Negro slaves in the United States. The Klan systematically lynched African-Americans who failed to recognize their "proper place in society," often inflicted grievous bodily harm upon them and sometimes burned their homes or businesses. The Nazi terrorism of the Jewish race, epitomized by Kristallnacht and culminating in the concentration camps, is another example. And South African apartheid was to some extent preserved by racial terrorism.

The most obvious wrong-making characteristic of racial terrorism as such is that it is an extremely serious kind of racial discrimination. Any and all racial discrimination is prima facie morally wrong because it is a violation of the human right to equitable treatment of the members of the victimized race. Violence or the threat of violence is inflicted upon most of its direct targets and terror created in its indirect targets simply because they are members of another race. But being of another race is not a just-making reason for being treated worse than those of the same race as the terrorists. Hence, it violates the fundamental moral right to equitable treatment, the right not to be treated worse than others who are similarly situated without a just-making reason. And it is a very serious violation of this moral right because of how much worse its victims are treated.

Typically, although not necessarily, racial terrorism oppresses the race terrorized. It then inflicts specific harms by denying or limiting the political power and economic opportunity of the subordinated race. The former renders the members of that race especially vulnerable, and the latter tends to reduce them to poverty or at least the lack of many of the necessities of a decent human life. Moreover, it denies or unduly limits their human rights to vote and stand for elections, to remunerative work, to education and to access to any place or service intended for public use. Thus, Racial Terrorism is always prima facie morally wrong because it violates the moral right to equitable treatment of the members of the terrorized race, and when it constitutes oppression, wrong because of the special harms it inflicts upon them and the human rights it violates. Ethnic terrorism, such as the ethnic cleansing that took place during the breakup of the former Yugoslavia, is prima facie morally wrong for analogous reasons.

2.9 Family Quasi-Terrorism

Claudia Card argues that family members sometimes, in fact far too often, become terrorists.

> Like other terrorists, abusive intimates use threats and heightened fear to manipulate and control. Spousal batterers use threats to obtain service and deference in everything from sex and money to petty details of household management. Physically and sexually abusive parents use terror to secure the silence and compliance of children, often compliance with wrongful demands (Card 2002, p. 143).

Wife battering or child abuse typically creates terror in its victim that is often used to coerce them into continuing compliance with the wishes of the abuser. This does not constitute terrorism as I now define it because strictly speaking there is no distinction between the direct target and the indirect target, the victim of violence and the person coerced are the same. Nevertheless, it is very similar because to standard cases of terrorism because violence is used or threatened against some present self in order to coerce his or her future self. Hence, it is useful to recognize it as quasi-terrorism. As such it has all the defining wrong-making characteristics of terrorism except that it does not use one person as a means of coercing another person.

The most obvious wrong-making characteristic of family terrorism is that it violates the terrorist's special duties, both moral and legal, to its victims. When one enters into a family partnership, not necessarily a formal marriage, one acquires moral responsibilities to one's partner, and by having a child, one acquires responsibilities of care for that child. To subsequently use or threaten violence against one's partner or child is, not only to fail to fulfill these family responsibilities, but to grievously violate them.

Family terrorism also harms the members of the family by destroying or severely damaging the trust and affection that makes intimacy possible. Intimate personal relationships have a very special value because they make possible the sharing of almost all aspects one's life, close reliable flexible cooperation, mutual caring and response to each others' needs, feelings and aspirations. Hence, any action that undermines intimacy is very harmful by destroying these precious values.

Family terrorism is often, fortunately not always, exceedingly harmful by inducing post-traumatic stress disorder in its victims.

> Judith Lewis Herman argues that the post-traumatic stress disorders of survivors of domestic violence and rape are importantly similar to the "shell shock" of World War I combat survivors. Finding that "the most common post-traumatic disorders are those not of men in war but of women in civilian life," she argues that women and children subject to civilian rape and domestic violence actually are in a war… (Card 2002, p. 144).

Family terrorism tends to produce this very harmful disorder precisely because it is perpetrated by a member of one's own family, someone to whom one has rendered oneself vulnerable by one's previous loving trust.

Finally, family terrorism is normally prima facie morally wrong because it reduces its victim to a condition of involuntary servitude (Card 2002, p. 143). Family terrorism uses or threatens violence against a family member in order to coerce him or her. Thus family terrorism typically produces an ongoing coercion that degrades the status of its victims. As family members coerced into submission, they are forced to serve their oppressors against their wills. And this constitutes a permanent or semi-permanent status of involuntary servitude, because they feel themselves unable to leave the oppressive relationship due to the threat of violence should they attempt to escape. Clearly, it is morally wrong to hold any human being in involuntary servitude, a status shockingly close to slavery.

Other examples of quasi-terrorism are not uncommon. For example, the school bully who picks on a classmate in order to scare him into regularly giving up some or all of his lunch money, or the employer or supervisor who harasses an employee into giving him sexual favors, or an individual or group of individuals who use or threaten violence against a neighbor, often someone suspected of being a sexual pervert or know to be of an "undesirable" race or religion, to terrorize him or her into leaving the neighborhood.

2.10 Conclusion

Terrorism, the attempt to coerce an indirect target by means of terror produced by the use or threat of violence against a direct target, is always at least prima facie wrong. This is because it has four essential wrong-making characteristics. It is coercive; it terrorizes; it uses or threatens violence; and it uses persons as means only. Although any species of terrorism is necessarily prima facie wrong for these four generic reasons, several species are especially immoral because of their distinctive wrong-making characteristics. Political terrorism undermines trust in a context of mutual dependence, puts liberal society into conflict with itself, undermines the individual and collective capacity for autonomous self-government, and disrupts the patterns of social activity that sustain the social order. State terrorism violates the moral duty of a nation state to protect its population from harm and violates their moral right to equitable treatment under law. International terrorism threatens the peace and security of the international community and violates the sovereignty or quasi-sovereignty of the invaded nations. Racial terrorism always violates the moral right to equitable treatment of members of the terrorized race, and often it inflicts the special harms of oppression and violates several human rights of the oppressed. The family quasi = terrorist violates his moral responsibilities to his victims, destroys the necessary conditions of intimacy, often causes post-traumatic stress disorder, and tends to reduce its victims to involuntary servitude. Whether, in spite of these very serious wrong-making characteristics, terrorism or quasi-terrorism could be morally justified under any circumstances remains to be seen.

But first I owe a brief explanation to my perceptive reader. I have not discussed several characteristics that are often believed to explain the immorality of terrorism, most notably that it is the use of violence against non-combatants or the innocent. I have ignored this consideration here because this is not why terrorism is, at least under normal circumstances, immoral. It is prima facie wrong because, among other things, the use or threat of violence inflicts harm and violates moral rights. The fact that it is often an attack on innocent persons or non-combatants is relevant to the moral assessment of terrorism in another way. It excludes one possible justification of terrorism, that terrorism is a defensive response to the wrongful aggression of its victims.

Tamar Meisels, among others, disagrees with my moral assessment. She takes its use of violence against the innocent as definitive of terrorism and the feature that explains why it is so seriously immoral.

> Terrorism, unfortunately, is alive and well, but so is its distinctiveness as a particular form of political violence, which can and should be strictly understood and morally condemned. Once again, terrorism is the intentional random murder of defenseless non-combatants, with the intent of instilling fear of mortal danger amidst a civilian population as a strategy designed to advance political ends.... Terrorism is a particularly morally objectionable form of free riding, as it relies inherently on the moral restraint of others and it is a paradigmatic instance of the ruthless use of individuals as mere means towards an end which they cannot conceivably share (Meisels 2008, pp. 52–53).

However, neither of these wrong-making characteristics depends upon the non-combatant status of the victims of terrorism, for they apply equally to attacks upon military personnel. For example, when Hezbollah terrorists attacked the marine barracks in Lebanon inflecting many casualties, they were using the individual marines as mere means in violation of their status as ends-in-themselves and relying upon the moral scruples of the United States not to retaliate with the indiscriminate use of its military force.

Similarly, the fact that non-state terrorists lack the authority to use violence that states possess or that terrorism is seldom if ever necessary because there are less harmful alternatives undermine potential justifications but are not themselves wrong-making features of terrorism. What, then, might justify terrorism?

References

Bauer M (2005) What is distinctive about terrorism? and what are the philosophical implications? In philosophy 9/11: thinking about the war on terrorism. In: Shanahan T (ed) Open court, Chicago and LaSalle, pp 3–22

Card C (2002) The atrocity paradigm: a theory of evil. Oxford University Press, Oxford

Goodin RE (2006) What's wrong with terrorism. Polity Press, Cambridge

Grovier T (2005) Physical violence in political contexts: grounds for a strong presumption against violence. In philosophy 9/11: thinking about the war on terrorism. In: Shanahan T (ed). Open Court, Chicago and LaSalle, pp 107–128

Hare RM (1979) On terrorism. J Value Inq 13:241–249

Kant I (1949) In critique of practical reason and other writings on moral philosophy. In: Beck LW (ed) University of Chicago Press, Chicago, pp 50–117

Leiser BM (1986) Liberty, justice, and morals: contemporary values conflicts, 3rd edn. Macmillan Publishing Company, New York

Meisels T (2008) The trouble with terror: liberty, security, and the response to terror. Cambridge University Press, Cambridge

Narveson J (1991) Terrorism and morality. In violence, terrorism, and justice. In: Frey RG, Morris CW (eds) Cambridge University Press, Cambridge, pp 116–169

Ruddick S (2003) The moral horror of the September attacks. Hypatia 18:212–222

Scheffler S (2006) Is terrorism morally distinctive? J Polit Philos 14:1–17

Wellman C (1961) The language of ethics. Harvard University Press, Cambridge

Wellman C (1982) Welfare rights. Rowman and Littlefield, Totowa

Wellman C (2005) Medical law and moral rights. Springer, Dordrecht

Chapter 3
How Could Terrorism Be Justified?

Abstract Terrorism cannot be justified either as he least harmful option or because it protects human rights alone because it both inflicts harms and violates human rights. However under very exceptional circumstances it might be justified when it both protects rights and prevents harms more than it violates rights and harms its victims. Although it cannot be justified merely because it equalizes rights violations, this may be a relevant consideration because the right to equitable treatment cannot be ignored in any possible justification. Terrorism could be justified because it liberates an oppressed people only if on balance it protects rights and prevents harms more fully than it violates rights and inflicts harms. It cannot be justified merely as an exercise of the right to self-determination or as a necessary means to a moral right because no moral right is absolute and unconditional. When terrorism is justified as a permissible tactic in a just war or as an exercise of the right to self-defense, this is because in this instance it protects rights and prevents harms more fully than it violates rights and inflicts harms. This might also be true when it is necessary to overcome an extreme emergency, although possibly an extreme emergency might exclude any judgment of wrongness without implying that terrorism is morally right. There is no objective evidence of any religious duty to engage in terrorism.

We have seen that there are four generic wrong-making characteristics of terrorism and that some of the most important species of terrorism have distinctive wrong-making characteristics that exacerbate their prima-facie wrongness. Given these facts, no one imagines that terrorism is ever morally innocent. However, this leaves open the question as to whether there are any contrary moral considerations that might, under special circumstances, cancel or outweigh the wrong-making characteristics of terrorism. How, if at all, could terrorism ever be justified?

3.1 The Least Harmful Option

Let us examine critically the most plausible justifications of terrorism. The most obvious reason that terrorism is prima facie wrong is that it causes serious harm. This suggests that terrorism is morally justified when it is the least harmful option, when the harm it causes is outweighed by the harms it prevents or the benefits it

C. Wellman, *Terrorism and Counterterrorism*, SpringerBriefs in Law 9,
DOI: 10.1007/978-94-007-6007-3_3, © The Author(s) 2013

produces. Hare argues that the ordinary person who is not a fanatic ought to reason about the justification of terrorism by weighing its costs and benefits.

> He will ask first of all what, in actual fact, the terrorist is doing when he commits a particular act. He is, say, killing a lot of people in an airport lounge with a sub-machine gun; he is bereaving their children and spouses (and bereavement is very often the greatest of human ills); he is wounding others; he is disrupting air travel, which may have far-reaching though hard-to-measure consequences if people who ought to go places decide not to for fear of such attacks; he is causing governments and airlines to spend a lot of money on precautions against terrorism, and so increasing taxes and the price of air travel; and so on. On the other hand, he is also (or so he thinks) helping to produce a state of affairs in which the cause he has embraced (say the expropriation of capitalists' wealth) is likely to be advanced (Hare 1979, p. 245).

Hare argues that one should assign weight to these various consequences by asking how much the interests of the victims or beneficiaries will be affected and how likely each of these various outcomes is. He concludes that no doubt some of the terrorist acts of members of the Resistance against the Germans during the Second World War could be justified by this utilitarian reasoning (Hare 1979, p. 247).

Although Kai Nielsen does not presuppose utilitarianism, he does argue that revolutionary terrorism could sometimes be justified by its moral consequences. To those who object that to engage in cost-benefit calculations when human lives are at stake is unjustifiably to play God, he replies that sometimes we have no alternative but to choose between evils. In such circumstances, a rational humane person ought to choose the lesser evil (Nielsen 1981a, p. 448). Therefore, he proposes a more complex least harmful option justification of terrorism. He argues that under exceptional circumstances, some acts of socialist revolutionary terrorism can be morally justified.

> Like all acts of violence in a political context, terrorist acts, if they are to be justified at all, are to be justified by their political effects and their moral consequences. They are justified when (a) they are politically effective weapons in the revolutionary struggle, and (b) when, everything considered, we have sound reasons for believing that, by the use of that type of violence, there will be less injustice, suffering and degradation in the world than if violence were not used or some other sort of violence were used. Surely, viewed in this light, terrorist acts are usually not justified, though in principle they could be and in some circumstances perhaps are, e.g. in the Algerian revolution against France, in the South Vietnamese resistance to American invasion and occupation, and in the revolutionary struggles of a few years ago in Mozambique and Angola (Nielsen 1981b, p. 39).

Although this proposed justification does not presuppose utilitarianism, it does appeal to the consequences of terrorism.

Following the lead of Herbert Marcuse, Nielsen explains his justification of revolutionary violence more fully earlier in his article.

> We must make rough historical calculations here. We must (1) consider 'sacrifices exacted from the living generation on behalf of the established society', (2) 'the number of victims made in defense of this society in war and peace, in the struggle for existence, individual and national', (3) consider the resources of the time—material and intellectual—which can be deployed for satisfying vital human needs and desires, (4) consider whether the revolutionary 'plan or program shows adequate promise of being able to substantially reduce the sacrifices and the number of victims' (Nielsen 1981b, p. 37).

These considerations could justify revolutionary violence if, but only if, its consequences are less harmful than any alternative course of action.

He concludes that the great English and French revolutions of the modern period were morally justified. He sums up the moral consequences of these revolutions in two rather different ways. He asserts that in spite of the terrible sacrifices exacted by them, these revolutions greatly enlarged the range of human freedom and happiness. He then asserts that, everything considered, the sum total of human misery and injustice has been lessened by them more than it could have been in any other achievable way. In addition to value consequences such as increased happiness and reduced misery recognized by utilitarianism, Neilsen grounds his justification on specifically moral consequences such as increased freedom and lessened injustice. And after describing a situation in which a small, impoverished, ill-educated ethnic minority suffers from gross discrimination, he suggests that it would be justified for them to engage in political violence to attain their human rights (Nielsen 1981b, p. 30).

Can these very different sorts of considerations be weighed against each other simply in terms of harms inflicted and harms prevented? I believe that they cannot. Even if one considers only distributive justice and defines this in terms of the distribution of benefits and harms, the fairness of any distribution is not simply a matter of maximizing benefits and minimizing harms. Indeed, this is the point of considering justice as well as utility in attempting to justify terrorism. And even if human rights, including the human right to freedom, are somehow grounded on human harms, respecting the human rights of individual persons cannot be reduced to any sum total of greatest benefits or least harms to everyone affected by one's action. Therefore, I do not believe that an act of terrorism could be justified simply by the fact that, under the circumstances, it is the least harmful act possible.

3.2 Protects Human Rights

If the least harmful alternative justification is inadequate because it ignores rights, perhaps terrorism is morally justified when it protects threatened human rights. In "Terrorism and Moral Rights," I quoted from a report in *Newsweek* of January 7, 1985:

> Last June the Ladies Center, the only abortion clinic in Pensacola, Fla., was demolished by a still unsolved predawn bombing. At 3:23 on Christmas morning, vigilantes struck again, detonating a bomb in the new Ladies Center offices near Pensacola regional Airport. Within 22 min, bombs also exploded in the offices of two local gynecologists who perform some abortions. Although no one was injured in the blasts, the offices of Dr. William Permenter were gutted by fire and the three explosions did an estimated $375,000 in damage. Permenter later said he would no longer perform in-office abortions and complained that no one would rent to him because of the insurance risk. But another victim, Dr. Bo Bagenholm, declared, "This isn't going to stop anything."

Presumably those who perpetrated these bombing would justify their actions by claiming that they were protecting the right to life of human fetuses. Similar reasoning is often used by animal rights terrorists.

After examining a number of ways in which this sort of justification can be challenged, I concluded:

> This writer remains firmly convinced that the recent antiabortion bombings in our country are morally wrong. But this is because the presuppositions of those who defend such bombings are not accepted. If the human fetus did have a full right to life, and if bombing so-called abortion clinics were an effective way to prevent or greatly reduce the number of abortions, and if this means of preventing abortions did not indiscriminately destroy very much untainted property or property of the innocent, then it would be morally justified. One can even dimly see the crucial elements in a plausible justification of such terrorism. It would not be a utilitarian justification that disregards or underestimates moral rights; it would be a rights-based justification. It would ground the right of the terrorists to bomb the clinics upon the more fundamental right—even the duty—to protect the moral rights of the potential victims of those who murder unborn children. It would not deny that the means used to protect moral rights harm, very seriously harm, many victims of the terroristic activity. But precisely because it takes rights seriously, it would not regard these harms as outweighing the right to life of the fetus (Wellman 1987, pp. 137–138).

Now, two decades later, I wonder why I was so confident that this sort of reasoning would justify terrorism.

Many acts of terrorism are morally wrong, not only because they violate human rights, but also because they inflict independent harms. No doubt the 9/11 attacks on the Twin Towers violated the rights to life and personal security of the many persons killed or injured that day and probably violated the property rights of the firms that occupied and the owners of the buildings. However, they seriously harmed many others in ways not reducible to rights-violations. They left many persons bereaved by the death of loved ones, but there is no human right not to be made bereaved. They caused the airlines and governments throughout the world to drastically increase security measures costing millions of dollars that reduced the profits of the airlines and increased the debts of nation states. They discouraged international travel to such a degree that the tourist industries in Europe and Asia lost considerable income, thus harming their owners and sometimes employees who lost their jobs. Therefore, any adequate justification of terrorism must consider both rights and harms.

3.3 Protects Rights and Prevents Harms

Accordingly, any sufficient justification of terrorism must be complex. To justify any act or campaign of terrorism one must show that the rights it protects and the harms it prevents are not outweighed by the rights it violates together with the harms it causes. Even ignoring the difficulty of knowing the full consequences of any act of terrorism, one must still overcome two serious problems of moral judgment.

First, how can one balance the weight or importance of one human right or set of rights against some conflicting right or set of rights? The obvious solution, and one sometimes proposed, is to rank-order human rights by their relative importance. It might seem that the human right to life always outweighs every other human right because without life, one cannot exercise or enjoy any additional rights. But the fact that life, remaining alive, is a necessary condition for the exercise or enjoyment of any or all of one's rights does not imply that the *right to* life is also a necessary condition. To be sure, if one's right to life is violated by being murdered, then one is also deprived of every right. However, one's right to life is also violated when one's life is merely endangered, and this might leave many of one's other human rights intact.

Some moral or political philosophers adopt a version of Henry Shue's distinction between basic human rights and non-basic rights.

> Basic rights, then, are everyone's minimum reasonable demands upon the rest of humanity. They are the rational basis for justified demands the denial of which no self-respecting person can be reasonably expected to accept. Why should anything be so important? The reason is that rights are basic in the sense used here only if enjoyment of them is essential to the enjoyment of all other rights. This is what is distinctive about a basic right. When a right is genuinely basic, any attempt to enjoy any other right by sacrificing the basic right would be quite literally self-defeating, cutting the ground out from under itself. Therefore, if a right is basic, other, non-basic rights may be sacrificed, if necessary, in order to secure the basic right (Shue 1980, p. 19).

Shue's assumption that there is a sub-set of human rights that are so interdependent that they are indivisible can and should be questioned (Nickel 2008, p. 990). Although there are other ways of explaining why basic human rights are more important than non-basic rights, this approach will not enable one to resolve conflicts between two or more basic human rights or between two or more non-basic rights.

Moreover, the attempt to rank-order human rights is fundamentally misguided. This is because the importance of any human right to its possessor varies depending upon the circumstances. The right not to be arbitrarily deprived of one's property is very important to a member of a racial minority living at the poverty line in a society that discriminates against persons of her race, but much less important when what is at stake is unjust taxation of the top ten percent of incomes over a million dollars. The right to liberty matters greatly to anyone under a government that detains large numbers of individuals suspected of opposing its regime but matters must less to a citizen of a society that respects due process. The human right to social security might be of little interest to a person with a reliable income and valuable investments that enable her to live in comfort but would be immensely valuable to a person so disabled that she is incapable of earning even a minimal income. What is necessary, therefore, is to evaluate the importance of each human right at stake to its possessor under the circumstances and to combine these evaluations in an overall judgment of which right or set of rights outweighs the others. There is no mathematical calculation that will yield a precise solution to any conflict of human rights. In many cases, one cannot be confident that one's comparative evaluation is correct. But sometimes it will be reasonably clear how one ought to act in a situation where human rights conflict. However, even when terrorism protects more important human rights than it violates, it may still be unjustified because of the harms it inflicts upon its victims.

Here one confronts a second difficult problem in moral theory and practice. How can one combine any conclusion about the relative weight of conflicting moral rights with any balancing of harms and benefits? Once more there is no easy solution to this problem. It is generally assumed that human rights have a high priority when weighed against other morally relevant considerations (Nickel 2007, p. 9). Some moral and political philosophers insist that they are so very important that they always trump any calculation of harms or benefits. But this assumption goes beyond the arguments of Ronald Dworkin who coined the slogan "Rights as Trumps" (Dworkin 1984, pp. 153–167). Although he insists that the moral rights implicit in the constitutional law of the United States (presumably human rights) cannot be grounded on overall utility or the balance of social benefits and harms, he recognizes that they are not absolute and might be justifiably infringed "to prevent a catastrophe, or even to obtain a clear and major public benefit…" (Dworkin 1977, p. 191). Therefore, the priority of human rights is not so very high that it excludes the moral relevance of other harms or benefits.

How, then, can one combine any weighing of violations of human rights with a balancing of additional harms or benefits resulting from an act of terrorism? In *Real Rights* I summed up my discussion of conflicts of moral rights as follows: "What I am suggesting is that one can and should weight conflicting rights against each other by weighing their grounds as these apply to or are qualified by the special circumstances of the case in question" (Wellman 1995, p. 233). Because human rights are grounded upon human values, although not simply maximum utility, there is a common denominator by which to judge the importance of rights violations and harms or benefits. Therefore, one can sometimes reach a fairly reliable conclusion about whether some act or campaign of terrorism is, given the circumstances, morally justified.

A plausible candidate for justification is the terrorism of the African National Congress against the practice of apartheid by the South African government. The ANC was a nonviolent organization until after the Sharpeville Massacre of 1960 in which the South African police killed 69 peaceful protesters and wounded over 180 others. From 1961 until 1989 it committed well over one thousand acts of terrorism. One of the largest attacks, and probably the most notorious, was the Church Street bombing in 1983. Although the target was the South African Air Force headquarters, the bomb exploded during rush hour killing 19 and wounding over 200 persons. This suggests that ANC terrorism typically violated the right to life of a significant number of victims, the right to personal security of many more, and the property rights of others. In addition, it harmed those who were bereaved or whose loved ones were injured as well as those affected by the loss of valuable property destroyed.

On the other hand, the human rights violated and the human harms inflicted by the South African government were vastly greater. Article II of the *International Convention on the Suppression and Punishment of the Crime of Apartheid* of 1973 charges that apartheid violates at least the human rights to life, to liberty, to freedom from torture or cruel, inhuman or degrading treatment or punishment, to work, to education, to a nationality, to freedom of opinion and expression, to freedom of peaceful assembly and association, to marriage, to equal protection of the laws, and to property. And P. Eric Louw reports many seriously harmful effects of apartheid suffered especially by those forcibly moved to the homelands. These include unemployment, inferior education, lack of adequate housing, deep poverty, often malnutrition, and the disruption of their traditional cultural patterns of life (Louw 2004). Although some would appeal to these past evils of apartheid to justify the ANC terrorism that eventually contributed to its elimination, this is not the relevant comparison.

The ANC terrorism was justified only if the rights violations and harms that it prevented outweigh the rights violations and harms inflicted by its violent attacks. One can make a moderately reliable estimate of the latter by examining the recorded facts about ANC terrorism. But the former requires one to judge how much longer apartheid would have continued unabated were there no or many fewer acts of terrorism. After all other relevant factors were nonviolent political activities within South Africa and external pressure, especially economic sanctions against it. Assuming that ANC terrorism was a significant force in eliminating apartheid, an assumption made plausible by the central role that the ANC played in the negotiations leading to this result, it appears that the ANC terrorism was in fact morally justified because of the way in which it protected human rights and prevented harms for millions of South Africans.

However, one should be cautious in judging that any act of terrorism is in fact morally justified both because of uncertainty about the facts of the case and because of the complexity of the moral reasoning required. It is a mistake to conclude that terrorism is justified simply because it is the least harmful option or because it protects human rights. One must weigh in the balance the harms and benefits resulting from terrorism against the harms eliminated by it together with the importance of the rights protected against that of the rights violated by it. Presumably it would be very difficult, although not on principle impossible, to justify an exceptional act or series of acts of terrorism in this manner.

3.4 Equalizes Rights Violations

Perhaps terrorism is morally justified when it equalizes rights violations. Virginia Held argues that:

> In a well-developed scheme of assured rights, rights should not be traded off against one another, or judged in comparative terms.... In a defective society, on the other hand, where rights are not in fact being respected, we should be able to make comparative judgments about which and whose rights violations are least justifiable. Was it more important, for instance, for blacks in South Africa to gain assurance of rights of personal safety than for white South Africans to continue to enjoy their property rights undisturbed? While blacks are denied respect for their most basic rights, it seems worse to continue these violations than to permit some comparable violations of the rights of whites participating in this denial (Held 2008, p. 82).

This example suggests that terrorism to decrease the violations of the human rights of black South Africans, even if it violates some of the human rights of white South Africans, might be less unjustified than refraining from this means of combating racial oppression.

Held then explains how this sort of justification rests on the moral principle of distributive justice.

> It seems reasonable, I think, that on grounds of justice, it is better to equalize rights violations in a transition to bring an end to rights violations than it is to subject a given group that has already suffered extensive rights violations to continued such violations, if the severity of the two violations is similar. And this is the major argument of this chapter. If we must have rights violations, a more equitable distribution of such violations is better than a less equitable distribution (Held 2008, p. 88).

Held concludes that terrorism cannot be ruled out as unjustifiable on a rights-based analysis any more than it can be on a consequentialist one (Held 2008, p. 89).

I agree that taking human rights seriously does not necessarily rule out the moral justification of terrorism, but I do not believe that terrorism could be justified simply because it is the only available way to equalize human rights violations. Terrorism is prima facie morally wrong, not only because it violates rights, but also because it imposes other kinds of serious harms upon its victims. Therefore, any justification of the sort that Held proposes would have to supplement its appeal to the just distribution of rights violations with some comparative judgment of the other harms and benefits resulting from terrorism. Virginia Held has oversimplified the reasoning required to justify terrorism.

But could she not reply that I have made the same mistake earlier in this chapter? When I concluded that one could justify terrorism by balancing the harms and benefits resulting from terrorism together with the importance of the rights protected and violated by it, I ignored the relevance of distributive justice to the moral status of terrorism. That distributive justice is sometimes relevant to the justifiability of terrorism is clearly shown by her discussion of the distribution of rights violations in an oppressive society such as South Africa. However, I suggest that distributive justice is not a third dimension in the moral evaluation of terrorism that needs to be added to my rights plus value results reasoning because it can be considered an implication of the human right to equitable treatment already included in the justification I have proposed.

3.5 Liberates an Oppressed Group

My reference to the hypothetical terrorism of the antebellum abolitionists and Held's reference to apartheid suggest that terrorism is morally justified when it liberates an oppressed group. And as a Socialist moral philosopher, Kai Nielsen writes:

> If one travels through Latin America (for example) and is even a tolerably careful observer and one supplements one's own observations with the reading (say) of Sven Lundqvist's perceptive and in-depth factual account of conditions there, and reads as well the interpretive writings of Salvador Allende and Carlos Marighela, the conclusion

> is unavoidable that the level of violent oppression of masses of people in Latin America is such as to make—as Marighela would put it—a commitment to revolution to achieve socialism the moral duty of a humane and informed human being, where there is some reasonable chance of its success (Nielsen 1981b, p. 52).

Why might the oppression of masses of people make revolutionary violence in the form of terrorism morally permissible, even a moral duty?

Presumably it has something to do with the fact that people are being oppressed. The *Oxford English Dictionary* defines the transitive verb "to oppress" in the relevant sense as "To keep (a person or group of people, esp. a minority or other subordinate group) in subordination and hardship by the unjust exercise of authority, power, or strength; to exploit; to tyrannize over." Perhaps it is the injustice of the exercise of authority or power that justifies terrorism to liberate the oppressed group. Paradigm cases would be the oppression of racial, ethnic, or religious minorities, and the injustice would consist in the fact that oppression would then consist in racial or ethnic or religious discrimination. No doubt any such discrimination is morally wrong. Probably it is a violation of the human right to the equal protection of the law or, more generally, the human right to equitable treatment. But how could this fact justify terrorism that by its very nature violates several human rights and in addition inflicts serious harms upon its victims? I cannot understand why terrorism is not at least as unjust to its victims as oppression is or how any appeal to the single human right to equal protection or equitable treatment, as important as it is, could justify the violation of a number of human rights and the infliction of serious harms.

Nielsen asserts that in Latin America "masses of people" are being oppressed. Being oppressed means being kept in subordination and hardship. And presumably subordination involves the violation of human rights and hardships are harms. Therefore, even though terrorism to liberate an oppressed group would violate the human rights of some persons and impose harms on some additional victims, these wrongs might be outweighed by the fact that it would protect the human rights and eliminate the hardships imposed on many more victims of oppression. But if true, this would not constitute a distinct kind of justification of terrorism based on the nature of liberation or oppression as such; it would be to describe one set of circumstances to which the complex weighing of rights violations and together with resulting harms and benefits applies.

However, Frantz Fanon suggests a justification of terrorism that is based upon the nature of oppression and the value of liberation. He believes that by their violent oppression, the colonial powers deny the human dignity of the colonized people they subjugate and thus damage or destroy their humanity.

> Native society is not simply described as a society lacking in values. It is not enough for the colonist to affirm that those values have disappeared from, or still better never existed in, the colonial world. The native is declared insensible to ethics; he represents not only the absence of values, but also the negation of values. He is, let us dare to admit, the enemy of values, and in this sense he is absolute evil (Quoted in Razack 2003, p. 204).

Because human dignity, the recognition of human beings as ends in themselves, is the essential condition of morality, liberation from oppression by any means is morally permissible.

Moreover, it is only by violence that the oppressed natives can reclaim their human dignity.

> To shoot down a European is to kill two birds with one stone, to destroy an oppressor and the man he oppresses, at the same time: there remain a dead man, and a free man....At the level of individuals, violence is a cleansing force. It frees the native from his inferiority complex and from despair and inaction, it makes him fearless and restores his self-respect (Fanon 1966, pp. 94, 122).

And if violence takes the form of systematic terrorism, it can liberate an oppressed people by forcing the colonists to recognize their humanity.

I doubt that terrorism can in fact achieve these moral goals. Unless individual acts of terrorism are morally justified on other grounds, engaging in them cannot restore the moral self-respect of the individual terrorists. And any systematic terrorism is more likely to confirm the prejudice of the oppressors that the natives lack moral value than to result in any recognition of their status as rational moral agent with human dignity. Moreover, human dignity does not consist in being recognized by others as a rational moral agent but in having and exercising the capacities for moral agency. This is why human dignity is inherent so that individual persons cannot be deprived of their human rights by the prejudices or mistreatment of their oppressors.

3.6 An Exercise of the Right to Self-determination

Article 2 of the United Nations *Declaration on the Granting of Independence to Colonial Peoples* of 1960 reads: "All Peoples have the right to self-determination; by virtue of that right they freely determine their political status, and freely pursue their economic, social and cultural development." Perhaps, then, terrorism is morally justified when it is an exercise of the fundamental moral right to self-determination.

The General Assembly resolution on measures to prevent international terrorism "*unequivocally condemns*, as criminal and unjustifiable, all acts, methods and practices of terrorism" but adds that the General Assembly:

> *Considers* that nothing in the present resolution could in any way prejudice the right to self-determination, freedom and independence, as derived from the Charter of the United Nations, of peoples forcibly deprived of that right...particularly peoples under colonial and racial regimes or other forms of alien domination....

What could justify the General Assembly from excluding violent acts of peoples exercising their right to self-determination from its condemnation of terrorism?

Perhaps the General Assembly intends to limit its justification to peoples under colonial and racial regimes or other forms of alien domination. If so, it probably implicitly presupposes that violence is morally justified when it liberates a people from domination or oppression. It makes this moral judgment consistent with its unequivocal condemnation of terrorism by defining international terrorism so as to exclude the exercise of the right to self-determination. On this reading, the right to self-determination would justify terrorism on my broader definition when, but only when, terrorism liberates a people from oppression. Therefore, this appeal to the right to self-determination adds nothing to the justification discussed in the previous section.

But the right to self-determination is often thought to apply to situations that do not involve either colonialism or racial oppression. It is frequently used to justify the demands of an ethnic minority to secede from a nation state or to a high degree of political autonomy within that state. Could the right to self-determination justify terrorism of a people under these circumstances? This depends upon the grounds of the right to self-determination. A people is most often defined as a group with a shared culture, typically including a common language, religion and even a set of moral standards. Accordingly, the right to self-determination of a people is thought to be grounded upon the immense value to individual persons of belonging to a people and identifying themselves as members of this ethnic group. Although this sort of reasoning has been advanced by a variety of moral and political philosophers and criticized by others, (Casals 2006, pp. 147–199) let us assume that it is valid. Still, I doubt that it would constitute an independent justification of terrorism. Surely nonviolent efforts to secede or achieve political autonomy are morally preferable to terrorism. But if they have failed or would, if attempted, fail, then only widespread terrorism would be likely to succeed. However, terrorism on this scale would violate several human rights and impose grievous harms on many victims. Therefore, once again the right to self-determination would not provide any distinctive moral justification for terrorism.

3.7 A Permissible Tactic in a Just War

Could terrorism be justified when used as a tactic in a just war? The usual examples are the British saturation bombing of German cities and the United States atomic bombing of Hiroshima and Nagasaki during World War II. These constitute terrorism because they used violence against the residents of the targeted cities in order to strike terror into the populations of Germany and Japan in order to cause their governments to surrender.

Since these were military actions taken in fighting a war, there can be no doubt that just war theory is applicable to them. And if the United Kingdom, the United States and their allies were engaged in a just war, then presumably the *jus ad bellum* criteria were satisfied. But what about the *jus in bello* criteria? These acts of terrorism surely violate the principle of discrimination, for they deliberately targeted non-combatants in order to maximize terror in the larger population. Some would reply that German and Japanese civilians were legitimate targets because they supported the unjust war of their governments. However, I would prefer to suggest that the principle of discrimination, a special case of the principle of double effect, is relevant to the moral character of the agents but not to the rightness or wrongness of their actions. Hence, to my mind, it is the principle of proportionality that is crucial. Here the question is whether these acts of terrorism shortened the war enough for the number of those killed, injured and caused to suffer together with the damage done by the bombing outweighed the numbers of those who would have been killed, injured and caused to suffer together with the damage that would have been done had the war continued somewhat longer. Although the factual information required to answer this question is not available, it seems possible that this could have been true regarding the saturation bombing of the German cities but, given the horrific effects of atomic bombs, highly unlikely in the case of the bombing of Hiroshima and Nagasaki. In any event, the conclusion to draw is that the principle of proportionality is decisive in determining whether terrorism can be morally justified as a tactic in what is, strictly speaking, a just war.

As war is defined in contemporary law, only military combat between nation states or civil revolutions within a state constitute war. But campaigns of terrorism by non-state actors are so prolonged, widespread and destructive of life, limb and property that they seem to be wars in a broader but entirely appropriate sense. Andrew Valls asks whether just war theory is applicable to this sort of terrorism and, if so, whether any such terrorism can be justified (Valls 2000, p. 65). Although whether such campaigns of terrorism should be classified as war or crime is controversial, it seems clear that they are so similar to warfare that they are prima facie wrong for very much the same reasons as war in the strictest sense. Hence, just war theory is presumably applicable to them.

Less easy to answer is the question of whether any campaign of violence by a non-state group could be morally justified? Well, if it is possible that terrorism could be a justified tactic in war a war between nation states, then why should one doubt that it could be justified when conducted by a non-state actor? Some would argue that non-state groups fail to satisfy the second *jus ad bellum* criterion of legitimate authority.

This requirement has traditionally been interpreted to imply that because the sovereignty of a state gives it a monopoly on the justified use of force, only states have the legitimate authority to wage war. But are states that seriously violate the human rights of its citizens or fail to protect them from avoidable harms morally legitimate?

> The considerations just advanced suggest that being a state is not sufficient for being a legitimate authority. Perhaps it is not necessary either. What matters is the plausibility of the claim to represent the interests and rights of the people. I would like to argue that some nonstate entities or organizations may present a very plausible case for being a people's representative….It must be emphasized that the position advocated here requires that the organization not only claim representative status but be perceived to enjoy that status by the people it claims to represent. This is a rather conservative requirement because it rules out "vanguard" organizations that claim representative status despite lack of support among the people themselves (Valls 2000, p. 71).

Hence, even if the sovereignty of a nation state does give it a monopoly on the legally justified use of force, it does not confer any monopoly on the morally justified use of force. Therefore, one should not assume that non-state actors lack legitimacy in the sense relevant to the criteria of a morally just war.

Once more, it is the criterion of proportionality that is decisive. Terrorism could be justified in a warlike context only if the importance of the human rights it violates together with the seriousness of the harms it inflicts do not outweigh the importance of the human rights it protects together with the magnitude of the harms it prevents. Only the importance of the interests and rights of a group of considerable size could ever be sufficient to justify terrorism, but this group need not be a people defined by their shared ethnicity. Although this sort of justification is possible in theory, I cannot think of a recent example that was justified in fact. In any event, this would not be a distinctive kind of justification because it would be only a special case of justification by protecting rights and preventing harms.

3.8 Self-Defense

The just cause most often given for going to war is self-defense, but terrorists sometimes justify their violence more generally on this basis. The obituary for Osama bin Laden in *Ihsan Magazine* begins with these words:

> To his enemies, whatever color or creed, he was a religious fanatic, a terrorist with the blood of thousands on his hands, a man who brought war and suffering to a broad swath of the Islamic world and came close to producing a global conflagration on a scale not seen for decades. To his supporters, whose numbers peaked in the few years after the attacks of 11 September 2001 in America that he masterminded, he was a visionary leader fighting both western aggression against Muslims and his co-religionists' lack of faith and rigour.

And an offshoot Al-Qaeda group proclaimed: "Do not cry for him….Instead rise and go on his path. Rise and thwart the American Zionist Western unjust aggression with all your power and energy." Implicit here is the claim that Muslim terrorism is justified as acts of self-defense against the continuing threat of aggression.

Because the United Nations has been unable to establish any precise definition of aggression, it is unclear when, if ever, international terrorism could be legally justified. However, what is at issue here is moral, not legal, justification. And Jean Combacau provides an illuminating remark that suggests a promising approach to this issue:

> In this context, the space for self-defence can only be limited: in fact it has the same role as it has in systems of national law, where subjects maintain the right to resort to force in reply to force, only in so far as the authority which legally holds the monopoly of the use of force is unable to ensure respect for that monopoly, that is, to prevent the use of force by the attacker (Combacau 1986, p. 10).

Since the common law was traditionally thought to reflect an underlying moral law, let us examine the right to self-defense in the Anglo-American law of torts.

There are three legal rules that define this right to self-defense. W. Page Keeton summarizes them as follows:

> The privilege of self-defense rests upon the necessity of permitting a person who is attacked to take reasonable steps to prevent harm to himself or herself, where there is no time to resort to the law….The privilege to act in self-defense arises, not only where there is real danger, but also where there is a reasonable belief that it exists….The privilege is limited to the use of force which is, or reasonably appears to be, necessary for protection against the threatened injury (Keeton 1984, pp. 124–126).

What could be the moral justification for this legal right to self-defense?

Any national legal system is morally justified by the fact that it is necessary to protect those subject to its jurisdiction from being harmed or having their moral rights violated. And this protection cannot be effective if individuals are permitted to attack one another whenever they see fit. Hence, normally a nation state has a moral justification for claiming a legal monopoly on the use of force. But when it is impossible for the state to protect a subject, its justification for prohibiting him or her from self-protection becomes inapplicable. Therefore, human beings, individually or collectively, have a moral right to a legal right of self-defense.

Note that the legal right of self-defense is limited, not by what the facts actually are, but by what it would be reasonable to believe that they are. I suggest that something similar is true of the moral right of self-defense. One has a moral liberty of using force to protect oneself when it is reasonable to believe that this is necessary to prevent serious harm to oneself or the violation of one of one's important moral rights. And one may use the degree of force that a reasonable person would believe to be necessary and proportionate. Why should reasonableness be the measure of this moral right? It is because to have a moral liberty of acting in some manner is by definition simply not to have any moral duty not to do so. And a duty-imposing moral reason is a dual-aspect reason, a reason for a moral agent to act or refrain from acting in some manner and for those in society with that agent to respond negatively in the event that he or she fails or refuses to conform to this reason (Wellman 1995, pp. 51–55). Finally, what justifies reacting negatively in such cases is the fact that failing to conform to the duty-imposing reason demonstrates a personality trait that undermines sociability, the ability to interact amicably and cooperatively with others. But as long as one acts reasonably, in the light of the reasons one believes to exist, one has not demonstrated any disregard for moral reasons and, thus, no unsociable character traits (Wellman 1995, pp. 85–88).

It appears that, at least in principle, some acts of terrorism could be justified as individual or collective exercises of the moral right to self-defense. But because the relevant moral reasons would be the harms and rights violations caused and prevented, it might seem to be simply a special case of the "protects rights and prevents harms" justification explained earlier in this chapter. However, whereas that justification rests on the actual balance of harms and rights violations, the appeal to the right to self-defense depends on what a reasonable person would believe about that balance. And there might be situations in which a reasonable person would believe that terrorism would protect rights and prevent harms to a greater extent than would actually be the case. However, I doubt that there would be many situations in which this would be true.

3.9 The Necessary Means to a Moral Right

Ted Honderich advances a simple but powerful justification for the contemporary Palestinian terrorism. The Palestinian people have a moral right to a viable national state of their own. Under present circumstances, the only possible means, the necessary means, for them to get such a state is terrorism. Therefore they have a moral right to engage in terrorism (Honderich 2008, pp. 14–16). This kind of justification could easily be applied to other instances of terrorism.

This justification rests upon the general principle that if one has a moral right to something, then one has a moral right to the only possible means to that thing. But is this merely an appeal to the principle that the end justifies the means? Not in the over-simple and disreputable version that holds that any good end, or at least any very good end, justifies any and every means to that end. It is not an appeal to value per se, but a more limited principle applying to moral rights only.

Here one needs to bear in mind that rights have a modality quite different from the degrees or relative amounts of value. What kind of a right might the moral right of the Palestinian people to a viable national state be? Well it might be a claim-right against the international community to be recognized as a state and granted all the legal rights of a nation state. But any such right would call for action by the international community, not permit the Palestinian people to take action into their own hands. If it is to justify engaging in terrorism, then it must be some sort of a liberty-right, a moral right to act in some specific manner. Presumably this would be either the moral right to strive for a viable national state or the moral right to achieve such a state. But terrorism could never be a necessary means to the former right, for there are always many possible ways to strive for statehood. Thus, only the moral right to achieve a viable national state could be relevant to a right to use terrorism as a necessary means to achieve this end.

Precisely how might a moral right to achieve a viable national state imply the moral right to use terrorism as a means? Honderich suggests an answer when he observes that terrorism often takes innocent lives, How, then, could it be justified as a necessary means? His answer is that both rights are grounded on the principle of humanity. Because he does not explain how this principle could ground either right, or indeed any right at all, I adopt a more general answer. Any ground sufficient to justify a moral right to achieve a national state would be sufficient to justify a moral right to use any means necessary to achieve this end. And this is true simply because rational action is the use of means to achieve one or more ends.

But would this be sufficient to justify killing innocent people? Not necessarily. Because no moral right is absolute, the implied right to use terrorism as a means is a prima facie right limited by a principle of proportionality. This is not simply that the value of the end must be greater than the disvalue of the means. It is something like the principle that the amount of harm done together with the importance of the rights violated must be less than the amount of good achieved and the importance of the moral right satisfied.

Accordingly, there are three conditions that must be satisfied if terrorism is ever to be justified by a right to use the necessary means to a prior moral right. First, can the use of terrorism ever be proportionate? I have argued in Sect. 3.2 of this chapter that under very special circumstances this condition might be satisfied.

Second, terrorism must be necessary, the only possible means to some prior moral right. Obviously there are always a wide variety of logically possible means to any assumed moral right, but what is required here is factual possibility in a strong sense. A possible means, in the sense presupposed by Honderich's principle, is one that in fact could succeed, that is has a reasonable chance of succeeding, as a means to the prior moral right. It is in this sense, that terrorism is sometimes defended on the ground that those who use it have no alternative, meaning no viable or practicable alternative. Under some circumstances it might be true that there is no viable alternative to terrorism, but it is equally true that only under very exceptional circumstances could terrorism itself be viable as a means to any prior moral right.

Third, terrorism must be a viable means to some independently justified moral right, and this right must be of sufficient importance to outweigh the rights inevitably violated by any act or campaign of terrorism. Perhaps a moral right to have a viable national state of one's own is this important, but one would like to see this shown by cogent moral reasoning, not just asserted dogmatically. In any event, it is clear that it would be very seldom, if even, that the use of terrorism could be justified as the necessary means to a moral right.

3.10 Necessary to Overcome a Supreme Emergency

Some moral philosophers have asked whether terrorism is justified when it is necessary to overcome a supreme emergency. Michael Walzer defends the terror bombing of German cities, at least early in World War II, because Britain was the only remaining obstacle to the subjugation of most of Europe by the Nazis. This was "an ultimate threat to everything decent in our lives, an ideology and practice of domination so murderous, so degrading even to those who might survive, that the consequences of its final victory were literally beyond calculation, immeasurably awful." Britain was facing a supreme emergency: an imminent threat of something utterly unthinkable from a moral point of view. Therefore, Britain was justified in violating the moral principle that civilians are inviolable in a just war. Although Walzer insists that terrorism is always morally wrong, others have suggested that his reasoning might be applicable to terrorist acts.

Precisely how might terrorism be justified when it is a response to a supreme emergency? Michael Walzer describes a supreme emergency as a threat of an evil "literally beyond calculation, immeasurably awful" (Walzer 2000, p. 253). If so, then one could not justify terrorism by the sort of weighing of the importance of human rights together with the balance of harms and benefits that I have previously described, for there can be no comparative weighing or balancing of immeasurable considerations. But if the evil threatened by a supreme emergency really is immeasurable, one could not know that it is great enough to justify terrorism. Therefore, one could never appeal to it to justify terrorism. I suggest that one should not take Walzer's description literally; one should interpret it as a hyperbolic assertion that in a supreme emergency the threatened evil is so immense that no calculation is required to see that it outweighs the importance of the rights that would be violated and the harms that would be inflicted by terrorism. On this interpretation, the appeal to supreme emergency is simply a special case, no doubt a very special and important case, of the weighing of rights and values that I have proposed.

There is, however, another interpretation of a supreme emergency that might provide a distinctive justification of terrorism. Igor Primoratz describes a supreme emergency as the threat of "something utterly unthinkable from a moral point of view" (Primoratz 2007, p. 17). Were this the case, then perhaps morality would become irrelevant and terrorism might be justified, not because it would be morally right but because it would not be morally wrong. Whether there could in fact ever be a threat of something morally unthinkable is highly uncertain. Possibly the threat of genocide or widespread ethnic cleansing would be so morally horrendous that no moral prohibitions would apply to those who resist it by any means available.

How could a supreme emergency render all moral prohibitions inapplicable? It might do so by threatening a Hobbesean state of nature, a condition in which cooperation and nonviolent coexistence would be impossible. Moral duties, including the duties not to violate human rights or inflict grievous harms on others, are grounded on duty-imposing moral reasons. These are dual-aspect practical reasons of a very special sort. They are reasons both for a moral agent to act or refrain from acting in some manner and for others to react negatively to anyone who acts contrary to them. And they are reasons for others to react negatively because by acting contrary to these reasons, a moral agent has shown himself to possess character traits incompatible with sociability factors, traits than enable individuals to interact in mutually rewarding ways or at the very least in nondestructive ways[1] (Wellman 1995, pp. 41–59). Thus, on my conception of moral reasons, moral duties could not hold in any situation where sociability has become impossible. Therefore, terrorism might be justified, or at least not unjustified, when one is faced with a supreme emergency that threatens this morally unthinkable condition.

3.11 A Religious Duty

Many persons of faith believe that terrorism is morally justified when it is a religious duty. For example Article Twelve of the *Hamas Charter* of August 1988 reads in part:

---

[1] See Carl Wellman, *Real Rights*, pp. 41–59.

> Hamas regards Nationalism as part and parcel of the religious faith. Nothing is loftier or deeper in Nationalism than waging Jihad against the enemy and confronting him when he sets foot on the land of the Muslims....While other nationalisms consist of material, human and territorial considerations, the nationality of Hamas also carries, in addition to all those, the all-important divine factors which lend to it its spirit and life; so much so that it connects with the origin of the spirit and the source of life and raises to the skies of the Homeland the Banner of the Lord....

Similarly Rabbi Meir Kahane called for the Israeli government to establish a Jewish terrorist group and subsequently asked:

> Have we so lost our bearings that we do not understand the ordained historical role of the State of Israel, a role that ensures that it can never be destroyed and that no further exile from it is possible? Why is it that we do not comprehend that *it is precisely our refusal to deal with the Arabs according to halakhic obligation that will bring down on our heads terrible sufferings, whereas our courage in removing them will be one of the major factors in the hurrying of the final redemption?* (Kahane 1981, p. 272)

And the Roman Catholic Church justified its inquisition as fulfilling its first and greatest duty to retain the faith given to it by God.

If the theological presuppositions of this reasoning are correct and if the commands of God do constitute the supreme moral standards and if God has in fact commanded terrorism, then religious terrorism could be and perhaps sometimes is morally justified. However, I am not a person who accepts any such faith. It is not that I have evidence to prove these articles of faith mistaken; it is simply that lacking evidence to prove them true, I remain an agnostic. Therefore, I do not believe that terrorism can be justified as a religious duty.

3.12 Conclusion

What should one conclude about the justifiability of terrorism? Because terrorism by its very nature violates human rights of and inflicts harms upon its victims, it is seldom if ever morally justified. An examination of the eleven most plausible proposed justifications reveals that the majority are inadequate. However, terrorism could on principle be justified when the importance of the human rights it protects together with the harms it prevents outweigh the importance of the human rights it violates together with the harms it causes. There seem to be a few very exceptional historical examples of terrorism that could were in fact be morally justified on this basis.

Similarly, a very few acts or campaigns of terrorism might be justified as exercises of the moral right to self-defense. However, this would be applicable to typical acts of terrorism only if aggression is defined more broadly than armed attack so that it includes any serious threat of harm or the violation of human rights. Although the right of self-defense is limited by a principle of proportionality, it is not measured in terms of actual consequences but by one's reasonable belief that the importance of the rights protected together with the harms prevented would outweigh the importance of the rights violated together with the harms caused by the terrorists.

It is also possible, although I suggest this very tentatively, that terrorism is justified, or at least not unjustified, when it is necessary to deal with a supreme emergency defined as the threat of a morally unthinkable situation. In such a case, the wrong-making properties of terrorism are not outweighed by its right-making properties, but the duties not to harm others and not to violate their human rights are undermined in a situation where sociability becomes impossible.

References

Casals NT (2006) Group rights as human rights. Springer, Dordrecht

Combacau J (1986) The exception of self-defense in U.N. practice. In: Cassese A (ed) Current legal regulation of the use of force. Martinus Nijhoff Publishers, Dordrecht, pp 9–38

Dworkin R (1977) Taking rights seriously. Harvard University Press, Cambridge

Dworkin R (1984) Rights as trumpts In jeremy waldron (ed) Theories of rights. Oxford University Press, New York

Fanon F (1966) The wretched of the earth. Grove Press, New York

General Assembly (1960) Declaration on the granting of independence to colonial countries and peoples. Yearbook of the United Nations 1960. Columbia University Press, New York, pp 49–50

General Assembly (1987) Resolution 42/159. Measures to prevent international terrorism. Yearbook of the United Nations 1987. United Nations, New York, pp 1063–1965

Hamas Charter (1988) Available on web at Hamas Charter

Hare RM (1979) On terrorism. J Value Inq 13:241–249

Held V (2008) How terrorism is wrong: morality and political violence. Oxford University Press, Oxford

Honderich T (2008) Terrorism in palestine. In: Law S (ed) Israel, Palestine and terror. Continuum Publishing Group, London, pp 3–16

Kahane M (1981) They must go. Grosset & Dunlop, New York

Keeton WP (1984) Prosser and keeton on the law of torts, 5th edn. West Publishing Co., Saint Paul

Louw PE (2004) The rise, fall, and legacy of apartheit. Praeger, Westport

Nickel JW (2007) Making sense of human rights. Blackwell Publishers, Oxford

Nickel JW (2008) Rethinking divisibility: towards a theory of supporting relations between human rights. Hum Rights Q 30:984–1001

Nielsen K (1981a) Violence and terrorism: its uses and abuses. In: Leiser BM (ed) Values in conflict: life, liberty, and the rule of law. Macmillan, New York, pp 435–470

Nielsen K (1981b) On justifying terrorism. Inquiry 24:21–57

Primoratz I (2007) Stanford Encyclopedia of philosophy. http//plato.stanford.edu/entries/terrorism/

Razack S (2003) Those who "Witness the Evil". Hypatia 18:204–211

Shue H (1980) Basic rights: subsistence, affluence and U. S. foreign policy. Princeton University Press, Princeton

Valls A (2000) Can terrorism be justified? In: Valls A (ed) Ethics in international affairs: theories and cases. Rowman & Littlefield, Lanham, pp 65–80

Walzer M (2000) Just and unjust wars: a moral argument with historical illustrations, 3rd edn. Basic Books, New York

Wellman C (1987) Terrorism and moral rights. In: Howie J (ed) Ethical principles and practices. Southern Illinois Press, Carbondale and Edwardsville, pp 128–153

Wellman C (1995) Real rights. Oxford University Press, New York

Chapter 4
International Responses

Abstract General Assembly resolutions first aimed to remove the causes of terrorism then later to eliminate it. The Security Council first imposed sanctions on states that failed to cooperate in the punishment of terrorism and later authorized the use of force against terrorists. United Nations conventions has criminalized several species of terrorism, but not terrorism in general. There is an emerging criminalization in customary international law. Several United Nations bodies supervise the ways in which nation states combat terrorism. These responses have been justified as necessary to protect human rights and preserve international peace. They have generally respected the sovereignty of nation states and the obligation to avoid any violation of the human rights of individual persons.

Although terrorism may once have been a domestic affair, taking place within and affecting only a single nation state, today it has taken on an international dimension. Even when terrorists operate within the territory of a single state, they are often inspired by foreign causes and trained in foreign countries. The most dramatic and harmful acts of terrorism are inflicted by the citizens of one country upon the nationals of another country and often facilitated or at least not obstructed by one or more third countries. Hence, terrorism is now of great concern to the international community.

The international community, as is name suggests, consists primarily of nation states, probably supplemented by other international organizations. These form a community insofar as they interact and share common interests. Although the international community encompasses more than its primary organization, the United Nations, the moral reasons that justify its responses to terrorism are suggested by the purposes proclaimed in the *United Nations Charter*. These are, briefly stated, to maintain international peace and security, to develop friendly relations among nations, to solve international problems of an economic, social, cultural or humanitarian character, and to promote respect for human rights and fundamental freedoms. Each of these is clearly relevant to international terrorism. Terrorism has led to war in Afghanistan and Iraq and in other areas of the Middle East and continues to threaten the security of Israel and Palestine. It disrupts friendly relations among nation states, the more positive aspect of international peace, and exacerbates

C. Wellman, *Terrorism and Counterterrorism*, SpringerBriefs in Law 9,
DOI: 10.1007/978-94-007-6007-3_4, © The Author(s) 2013

disputes that might otherwise be amicably and justly resolved. It most often occurs within the context of poverty, social or cultural alienation and imposes widespread suffering upon humanity. Finally, terrorist acts typically violate the human rights to life, personal security, liberty or property of its victims, and national responses to it often threaten the human rights to liberty, personal security, privacy and due process of those suspected of engaging in or even inadvertently abetting terrorism. And because of the importance of the purposes of the United Nations in preventing human suffering, increasing human welfare and protecting human rights, they justify the international community in responding to international terrorism by taking measures to prevent and eliminate it.

However, these justifications are only prima facie. There are other morally relevant considerations that may override them and thus render some contemplated responses morally unjustified. Let us identify some of the more important responses of the international community and assess their moral limits. To simplify exposition and avoid redundancy, I will limit myself to global international responses. Although regional responses are sometimes more effective and often more desirable, their justification and the moral limits to them are much the same as those applicable globally.

4.1 General Assembly Resolutions

There is a striking contrast between typical state responses to terrorism and the response of the General Assembly in its first resolution concerning terrorism. Nation states attempt to eliminate terrorism by gathering intelligence concerning potential terrorist attacks, detaining those who have or might in the future engage in terrorism, and punishing terrorists and those who aid or abet terrorism. They seldom make any serious effort to eliminate or even alleviate the real or alleged injustices that produce terrorism. However, Resolution 3034 (XXVII) of 1972 aims to prevent terrorism primarily by finding just and peaceful solutions to its causes rather than by counter measures. Thus operative paragraph 2 "*Urges* States to devote their immediate attention to finding just and peaceful solutions to the underlying causes which give rise to such acts of violence" and paragraph 6 "*Invites* States to take all appropriate measures at the national level with a view to the speedy and final elimination of the problem…" Notice both that it invites states to take action to eliminate the problem, not to eliminate acts of terrorism, and that it proposes measures only at the national level, not the introduction of new international measures. What explains this focus of the response of the General Assembly?

The General Assembly indicates one explanation in its preamble to Resolution 3034 by "*Recalling* the Declaration on Principles of International Law concerning Friendly Relations and Co-operation among States in accordance with the Charter of the United Nations" (General Assembly 1970, p. 788). It intends to justify its response by appealing to one of the purposes of the United Nations: "To develop friendly relations among nations based on respect for the principle of equal rights and self-determination…" (United Nations 1945, Article 1.2). However, it also intends to pursue this purpose by acting in accordance with the principle that "Nothing contained in the present Charter shall authorize the United Nations to intervene in matters that are essentially within the domestic jurisdiction of any State…" (United Nations 1945, Article 2.7). Indeed, the *Declaration on Friendly Relations* affirms the importance of this principle for its purpose.

> *Convinced* that the strict observance by States of the obligation not to intervene in the affairs of any other State is an essential condition to ensure that nations live together in peace with one another, since the practice of any form of intervention not only violates the spirit and letter of the Charter, but also leads to the creation of situations which threaten international peace and security (General Assembly 1970, p. 789).

Therefore, at least in 1970, the General Assembly believed that it ought to limit its response to international terrorism by the principle of non-intervention.

Leaving aside the legal status of this principle, what are its moral grounds? One morally relevant consideration is that intervention by one state or group of states in the affairs of any other state always renders cooperation in the pursuit of common interests more difficult and if serious, threatens international peace. Since international peace and cooperation are vitally important for the international community, this reason has great moral force. Another morally relevant consideration is that intervention in the affairs of any state is incompatible with its external sovereignty, its independence in governing those subject to its jurisdiction. External sovereignty is valuable to any state because interference by others in its governance undermines its ability to exercise its internal sovereignty, its right to govern its subjects. And its internal sovereignty is in turn justified as a necessary condition for effectively protecting those living within its territory from serious harm and the violation of their human rights. Hence, this consideration also has considerable moral force.

However, these considerations did not really require the General Assembly to abstain from more forceful measures to counter international terrorism. For one thing, international terrorism was and increasingly is a threat to international peace and a serious disruption of the friendly relations between nations that enable them to cooperate for humanitarian ends. These facts will often outweigh any damage to peace and friendly relations that moderate forms of intervention would create. For another thing, the morally justified principle of non-intervention prohibits only intervention in the domestic affairs of a nation state. But because international terrorism violates human rights and undermines international peace, both legitimate concerns of the international community, it is not a purely domestic affair. Therefore, although the principle of non-intervention does impose one moral limit on any justified responses of the international community to terrorism, this limitation is not as severely restrictive as the General Assembly assumed in 1972. At the very least, it did not require the Resolution 3034 to affirm merely that "*The General Assembly…Expresses deep concern* over increasing acts of violence which endanger or take innocent human lives or jeopardize fundamental freedoms" (General Assembly 1972, p. 650). It could and probably should have condemned such acts just as it did condemn "the continuation of repressive and terrorist acts by colonial, racist and alien regimes…" (General Assembly 1972, p. 650).

In Resolution 3034, the General Assembly indicates a second explanation of its reluctance to condemn all acts of terrorism or to advocate counter measures to eliminate them as follows:

> *The General Assembly,...Reaffirms* the inalienable right to self-determination and independence of all peoples under colonial and racist régimes and other forms of alien domination and upholds the legitimacy of their struggle, in particular the struggle of national liberation movements, in accordance with the purposes and principles of the Charter and the relevant resolutions of the organs of the United Nations (General Assembly 1972, p. 650).

Because members of national liberation movements exercising their right to self-determination often use the same violent tactics as those who perpetrate the "acts of violence directed at national leaders, diplomatic envoys, international passengers and other innocent civilians" that the Secretary General had in mind in proposing this item, (United Nations 1972, p. 639) any condemnation of all acts of violence might be misinterpreted to apply to the legitimate struggle for liberation from alien domination. And measures designed to counter acts of violence directed at innocent persons might be misapplied to individuals and organizations exercising the right of their people to self-determination.

The moral grounds of the right to self-determination are suggested by its development in international law. Article 1.2 of the *United Nations Charter* of 1945 declares a fundamental purpose of the United Nations to be "To develop friendly relations among nations based on respect for the principle of equal rights and self-determination of peoples, and to take other appropriate measures to strengthen peace." One ground of the right to self-determination is that if respected, it promotes the friendly relations among nations required for international cooperation in the pursuit of common values and that its violation at least threatens international peace and may even result in war.

The *Declaration on Granting Independence to Colonial Countries and Peoples* of 1960 reiterates this moral ground and postulates another:

> *Convinced* that the continued existence of colonialism prevents the development of international economic co-operation, impedes social, cultural and economic development of dependent peoples and militates against the United Nations ideal of universal peace,... (General Assembly 1960, p. 49).

A second ground of the right to self-determination is that its denial typically results in poverty and deprivation for the people living under alien domination.

Although the right to self-determination is not a human right because it is a group right of peoples not of individual human beings, it is asserted in Article 1 of both the International Covenants intended to give legal status to the rights merely proclaimed in the *Universal Declaration of Human Rights*. In its General Comment 12 the Human Rights Committee explains that:

> The right of self-determination is of particular importance because its realization is an essential condition for the effective guarantee and observance of individual human rights and for the promotion and strengthening of these rights. It is for that reason that States set forth the right of self-determination in a provision of positive law in both Covenants and placed this provision in article 1 apart from and before all the other rights in the two Covenants (Human Rights Committee 1984, para. 1).

Thus, a third and probably the most important moral ground of the peoples' right to self-determination is that if respected, it renders the exercise and enjoyment of human rights more secure and that its denial normally leads to the violation of the fundamental moral rights of individual persons. These three moral considerations, of which the General Assembly was well aware, explain why it assumed that the violent acts of those struggling for liberation from alien domination ought not to be condemned, much less eliminated.

Because the right of any people to self-determination is morally justified, those struggling for national liberation are often morally justified in using violent tactics in exercising this right. However, it does not follow that every violent action claimed to be an exercise of this right is justified. No moral right is absolute. Violent tactics ought not to be employed in the struggle for national liberation when they inflict serious harm on innocent persons without significantly advancing that cause or when their violation of the human rights of their victims is disproportionate to their contribution to that cause. The General Assembly ought to have condemned such violent actions and not insinuated that every violent act in the struggle for national liberation is morally innocent. Although the right to self-determination does constitute one limit on its response to terrorism, it did not apply that limit correctly by distinguishing between morally legitimate and illegitimate acts of violence.

It attempted to draw this line during the drafting of Resolution 3034 by defining international terrorism so as to exclude morally justified exercises of the right to self-determination, but it failed to reach agreement on this matter. In presenting his report on his preparatory consultations with members of the Sixth Committee, its chairman expressed the view that:

> The most difficult question remained that of defining the concept of international terrorism: all Members were in principle prepared to condemn international terrorism, but it appeared impossible to do this without identifying the phenomenon more precisely (United Nations 1972, p. 641).

No doubt the primary difficulty was political, the conflicting positions of the Western Powers intent on eliminating violent attacks on their national interests and the African and Asian countries struggling to achieve greater freedom from domination by and equality with the nation states with predominant power in international affairs. However, a second and more fundamental difficulty remained. Whether some violent act intended to further a morally justified cause is itself justified depends upon the circumstances. Therefore, it is impossible to formulate any moral principle that distinguishes, with precision and without qualification, between justified and unjustified acts of violence.

How, then, ought the General Assembly to have formulated its Resolution 3034? It probably responded to international terrorism more appropriately in its Resolution 40/61 of 9 December 1985. In the preamble to this resolution, the General Assembly reaffirmed the principle of self-determination in the Charter of the United Nations and also reaffirmed the inalienable right to self-determination and independence of all peoples. However, paragraph 1 of the operative provisions, "*Unequivocally condemns*, as criminal, all acts, methods and practices of terrorism wherever and by whomever committed, including those which jeopardize friendly relations among States and their security" (General Assembly 1985, p. 1169). To be sure, this utterly fails to draw the line between those morally unjustified acts of terrorism that ought to be condemned and legally prohibited and the legitimate violent acts of those exercising the right to self-determination that the international community ought to support rather than suppress. However, this is not a failure of the General Assembly, for it recognizes that this line needs to be drawn by other institutions of the international community, those that constitute the primary sources of international law and eventually the courts that apply this law to particular cases after considering the special circumstances of each case.

In later resolutions such as Resolution 49/60 of 9 December 1994, the General Assembly turned its attention from measures to prevent terrorism, primarily by removing its causes, to measures to eliminate terrorism by counter measures. Do these later resolutions exceed the moral limits imposed by either the right to self-determination or the principle of non-intervention? Not necessarily. Thus, paragraph 5 of the annex to this resolution asserts that:

> States must also fulil their obligations under the Charter of the United Nations and other provisions of international law with respect to combating international terrorism and are urged to take effective and resolute measures in accordance with the relevant provisions of international law and international standards of human rights for the speedy and final elimination of international terrorism... (General Assembly 1994, p. 1294).

Since the right to self-determination was recognized in the Charter and subsequently became established in international law, the General Assembly here requires only counter measures that do not violate the right to self-determination.

And paragraph 5 (a) urges states:

> To refrain from organizing, instigating, facilitating, financing, encouraging or tolerating terrorist activities and to take practical measures to ensure that their respective territories are not used for terrorist installations or training camps, or for the preparation or organization of terrorist acts intended to be committed against other states or their citizens (General Assembly 1994, p. 1295).

Counter measures such as these clearly conform to, in fact are specific applications of, the principle of non-intervention. Thus the transition from measures to prevent to measures to eliminate terrorism remains within these two moral limits on justified responses by the international community.

However, the most important moral limits on state responses to terrorism are the human rights possessed by all persons, even those suspected of or engaged in terrorism. The General Assembly (2004) has recognized the relevance of human rights both to terrorism and to counter-terrorism on a number of occasions, for example in the preamble to its Resolution 59/191 of 20 December 2004.

> *Reaffirming* that acts, methods and practices of terrorism in all its forms and manifestations are activities aimed at the destruction of human rights, fundamental freedoms and democracy, threatening the territorial integrity and the security of States and destabilizing legitimately constituted Governments, and that the international community should take the necessary steps to enhance cooperation to prevent and combat terrorism.

Noting the declaration on the issue of combating terrorism contained in the annex to Security Council (2003) resolution 1456 of 20 January 2003, in particular the statement that States must ensure that any measures taken to combat terrorism comply with all their obligations under international law and should adopt such measures in accordance with international law, in particular international human rights, refugee and humanitarian law.

Accordingly, the General Assembly resolved that: "States must assure that any measure taken to combat terrorism complies with their obligations under international law, in particular international human rights, refugee and humanitarian law." Its use of the word "must" implies the legal obligations of States under international law, reflecting the moral obligation to respect the human rights of everyone affected by their actions. Thus, the General Assembly limits its assertion that States must adopt measures of counter-terrorism to protect the human rights of its potential victims by insisting that all such measures must not violate human rights. Therefore, the most important General Assembly resolutions concerning terrorism remain within the limits of moral justification.

4.2 United Nations Conventions

Another kind of response to terrorism by the international community consists of conventions sponsored by the United Nations. Because treaties agreed by nation states are a primary source of international law, these conventions directly impose legal obligations and confer legal rights on the international level. And because they require state parties to take legal measures to prevent or eliminate terrorism, they also bring about obligations and rights in national legal systems. It is these counter measures by nation states that give the greatest force to these international conventions.

Article 53 of the *Vienna Convention on the Law of Treaties* points to one moral limit to any justified convention against terrorism as follows:

Treaties conflicting with a peremptory norm of international law (jus cogens).

A treaty is void if, at the time of its conclusion, it conflicts with a peremptory norm of general international law. For the purposes of the present Convention, a peremptory norm of general international law is a norm accepted and recognized by the international community of States as a whole as a norm from which no derogation is permitted and which can be modified only by a subsequent norm of general international law having the same character (United Nations 1969).

Peremptory legal norms of this character are controversial because they limit the ability of nation states to make international law by consenting to a proposed treaty and thus are inconsistent with the traditional doctrine that all international law derives its authority from the consent of those states that are subject to it. However, the International Law Commission has asserted the emergence of rules having the character of *jus cogens*, (International Law Commission 1966, pp. 247–249) and the majority of jurists now agree with its conclusion.

What are the moral grounds of peremptory norms in general international law? One kind of ground is suggested by Justice Tanaka in his dissenting opinion in the *South West Africa Cases* (*Second Phase*):

> If we can introduce in the international field a category of law, namely *jus cogens*, recently examined by the International Law Commission, a kind of imperative law which constitutes the contrast to the *jus dispositum*, capable of being changed by way of agreement between States, surely the law concerning the protection of human rights may be considered to belong to *jus cogens* (International Court of Justice 1966, p. 298).

But why might human rights justify a peremptory legal norm immune from modification by the consent of nation states? The most plausible explanation occurs in a later judgment of the International Court of Justice:

> In particular, an essential distinction should be drawn between the obligations of a State towards the international community as a whole, and those arising vis-à-vis another State in the field of diplomatic protection. By their very nature the former are the concern of all States. In view of the importance of the rights involved, all States can be held to have a legal interest in their protection; they are obligations *erga omnes* (International Court of Justice 1970, p. 3).

The court then gives as examples international legal norms prohibiting aggression or genocide and also principles concerning the basic rights of persons, including protection from slavery and racial discrimination. What morally justifies the peremptory character of these legal norms is that they are important to the international community as a whole and in the interest of every member state.

Morally justified peremptory norms of general international law constitute a generic moral limit to justified conventions because they limit the validity of any convention, whatever its subject, as an international treaty. Those who drafted the United Nations (1963) conventions against terrorism were well aware of this and respected these *jus cogens* norms. One can see this, not only in what they did not include in these treaties, but also in some of their provisions. Most notably, Article 2 of the *Tokyo Convention* of 1963 reads:

> Without prejudice to the provisions of Article 4 and except when the safety of the aircraft or of persons or property on board so requires, no provision of this Convention shall be interpreted as authorizing or requiring any action in respect of offenses against penal laws of a political nature or those based on racial or religious discrimination.

This article is intended to ensure that those applying the convention will not violate the peremptory norm against racial or religious discrimination. This morally justified norm is reflected similarly in Article 9 of the *Convention Against the Taking of Hostages* of 1979 and again in Article 15 of the *Convention for the Suppression of the Financing of Terrorism* of 1999.

More interesting and controversial are the specific moral limits on justified conventions typically grounded on one or a few human rights. A relevant example is the human right to asylum. Article 14 of the *Universal Declaration of Human Rights* defines this right as follows:

1. Everyone has the right to seek and enjoy in other countries asylum from persecution.
2. This right may not be invoked in the case of prosecutions genuinely arising from non-political crimes or from acts contrary to the purposes and principles of the United Nations (General Assembly 1948, p. 536).

The moral ground of this right lies in the nature of persecution, the evil from which a refugee seeks asylum. Persecution consists in oppressing or harassing someone, especially because of race, religion, or political action. Thus, it is a serious kind of discrimination. But what is morally wrong with discrimination? Article 1.1 of the *International Convention on the Elimination of All Forms of Racial Discrimination* of 1966 reads:

> In this Convention, the term 'racial discrimination' shall mean any distinction, exclusion, restriction or preference based on race, colour, descent, or national or ethnic origin which has the purpose or effect of nullifying or impairing the recognition, enjoyment or exercise, on an equal footing, of human rights and fundamental freedoms in the political, economic, social, cultural or any other field of public life (United Nations 1966b).

Accordingly what is morally wrong with discrimination, and presumably persecution, as conceived by the United Nations is that it nullifies or impairs the enjoyment or exercise of the human rights of its victims. And the human right to asylum is grounded upon the urgent need of anyone subjected to persecution to escape from this moral evil.

The right to asylum is relevant to any convention against terrorism because it will require State Parties either to extradite or prosecute anyone suspected of a terrorist offense specified in that treaty. However, this duty to extradite ought not to be exercised in a way that violates the suspect's human right to asylum. Hence, Article 15 of the *International Convention against the Taking of Hostages* limits the duty to extradite as follows:

> The provisions of this Convention shall not affect the application of the Treaties on Asylum, in force at the adoption of this Convention, as between the States which are parties to those treaties; but a State Party to this Convention may not invoke those Treaties with respect to another State Party to this Convention which is not a party to those treaties (United Nations 1979).

This article was the subject of prolonged debate during the drafting of this convention because it involves a delicate balancing between the urgent need to ensure that those who commit terrorist acts are punished and the need to protect potential victims of persecution from unjust punishment (United Nations 1979, p. 1139). This compromise formulation does not completely solve that moral problem because it restricts the applicability of the human right to asylum to its recognition in previously adopted treaties.

Another and more important human right, the right to property, is also relevant to the *International Convention for the Suppression of the Financing of Terrorism.* Article 8.1 reads as follows:

> Each State Party shall take appropriate measures, in accordance with its domestic legal principles, for the identification, detection and freezing or seizure of any funds used or allocated for the purpose of committing the offences set forth in article 2 as well as the proceeds derived from such offences, for the purposes of possible forfeiture (United Nations 1999).

The problem is that any such funds will be the property of some individual or organization. Hence, to freeze these funds would be to deprive the owners of the use of their property and to seize them would be completely to deprive the owners of their property. This need not be unjust were the owners actually guilty of using or intending to use their property to finance terrorism. But it would be unjust to freeze or seize their property merely on the suspicion that the owners are guilty of this offence. Article 17 of the *Universal Declaration of Human Rights* reads:

1. Everyone has the right to own property alone as well as in association with others.
2. No one shall be arbitrarily deprived of his property(General Assembly 1948, p. 537).

However, in order to ensure that any action to freeze or seize property that might be used to finance terrorism is not arbitrary, there must be some provision in the law that distinguished clearly between terrorism and other activities, such as the charitable work of many Islamic organizations. At this point, the failure of the United Nations to agree upon any definition of terrorism poses a serious problem.

The *International Convention for the Suppression of the Financing of Terrorism* addresses this problem in Article 2:

> Any person commits an offence within the meaning of this Convention if that person by any means, directly or indirectly, unlawfully and willfully, provides or collects funds with the intention that they should be used or in the knowledge that they are to be used, in full or in part, in order to carry out:
>
> (a) An act which constitutes an offence within the scope of and as defined in one of the treaties listed in the annex: or
>
> (b) Any other act intended to cause death or serious bodily injury to civilian, or to any other person not taking part in the hostilities in a situation of armed conflict, when the purpose of such act, by its nature or context, is to intimidate a population, or to compel a government or an international organization to do or abstain from doing any act (United Nations 1999).

The nine treaties listed in the annex are all the previous United Nations conventions and protocols designed to eliminated, or at least reduce, acts of terrorism. Because none of them attempted to define terrorism, this enabled the convention to specify many acts of financing terrorism without defining terrorism itself. However, in order to make the covenant applicable to others kinds of relevant acts, Article 2(b) fills the gap left by the absence of any established general definition of terrorism by a quasi-definition. In this way, it attempts to respect, as well as possible under the circumstances, the human right to property.

Another fundamental human right that limits any justified treaty is the right to liberty. Article 9.1 of the *International Covenant on Civil and Political Rights* asserts that: "Everyone has the right to liberty and security of person. No one shall be subjected to arbitrary arrest or detention. No one shall be deprived of his liberty except on such grounds and in accordance with such procedure as are established by law" (United Nations 1966a). Here also the lack of any established definition of terrorism threatens to render any arrests for the offence of financing terrorism arbitrary. Presumably, this threat is eliminated, or at least drastically reduced, by provisions (a) and (b) described above. Thus, this convention does reasonably well in respecting the moral limit imposed by the human right to liberty.

It also attempts to respect the human rights to due process asserted in Article 14 of the *International Covenant on Civil and Political Rights*. Thus, Article 17 reads:

> Any person who is taken into custody or regarding whom any other measures are taken or proceedings are carried out pursuant to this Convention shall be guaranteed fair treatment, including enjoyment of all rights and guarantees in conformity with the law of the State in the territory of which that person is present and applicable provisions of international law, including international human rights law (United Nations 1966a).

However, due process rights are not always effectively protected in the legal procedures of many nation states, and it would have been better to have specified the most important due process rights rather than to refer generally to "international human rights law." Perhaps the weakness of Article 17 reflects an undue regard for national sovereignty.

Still, national sovereignty is in most cases morally justified because it is a necessary condition any nation state to protect the human rights of its citizens and to effectively protect them from other serious harms. Hence, it constitutes another moral limit on any justified treaty. Most of the United Nations (2005) conventions against terrorism are drafted with this in mind. This restraint is seen most clearly in the *International Convention for the Suppression of Acts of Nuclear Terrorism* of 2005. Thus Article 3 reads:

> This Convention shall not apply where the offence is committed within a single State, the alleged offender and the victims are nationals of that State, the alleged offender is found in the territory of that State and no other State has a basis under article 9, paragraph 1 or 2, to exercise jurisdiction, except that the provisions of Articles 7, 12, 14, 15, 16 and 17 shall, as appropriate, apply in all cases (United Nations 2005).

And Article 22 specifies that: "Nothing in this Convention entitles a State Party to undertake in the territory of another State Party the exercise of jurisdiction and performance of functions which are exclusively reserved for the authorities of that other State Party by its national law." These provisions explicitly respect the mortal limits imposed by national sovereignty implicitly respected by the other conventions against terrorism by omitting provisions that would violate this limit.

A final moral limit relevant to conventions against terrorism is suggested, but not identified clearly, by the concept of a political offense. Antje C. Petersen reports:

> Extradition treaties play a particularly important role in the cooperative efforts to combat terrorism. Yet their effectiveness has been hampered by the fact that the political offense exception, contained in all extradition treaties, protects from extradition political offenders of all types, nonviolent and violent alike, including terrorists. In response to this dilemma, the United States and the United Kingdom recently signed a Supplementary Treaty exempting a number of violent crimes from the protection of the political offense exception (Petersen 1992, p. 767)

Article 14 of the *Convention for the Suppression of the Financing of Terrorism* similarly stipulates that "None of the offences set forth in article 2 shall be regarded for the purposes of extradition or mutual legal assistance as a political offence…" (United Nations 1999). Does this violate the moral limit indicated, but not defined, by the political offense exception?

The answer to this question is controversial both because the concept of a political offense is vague and because it is not clear what moral reasons there are for excepting political offenders from extradition. Petersen explains that:

> One of the most difficult questions connected to the political offense exception is how to determine what crimes are considered to be political offenses. Political offenses are generally divided into two kinds: "pure" political offenses (treason, sedition, and espionage), for which a political offense exception appears most sensible; and "relative" political offenses. Relative political offenses are "ordinary," often violent crimes that occur in connection with political uprisings (Petersen 1992, p. 775).

The difficulty is that violent acts of terrorism are often motivated by a political cause but do not occur in connection with a political uprising. Ought they, then, to be treated as political crimes for the purposes of extradition?

This depends on the moral reasons for including a political offenses exception in extradition treaties. Once more Petersen is helpful:

> One of the most frequently mentioned reasons for not extraditing persons accused of political crimes is the fear that the requesting state's judicial system will be incapable of treating justly those who have shown their disregard for or distrust of their government. Requested states may also fear that political offenders will be subjected to torture and other inhumane treatment in the requesting country (Petersen 1992, p. 776).

In short, the moral reason to refuse to extradite persons accused of political offenses is to protect them from the violation of their human rights, especially their rights to due process, personal security, freedom of expression, and freedom of association. That they need such protection is shown by how those accused of political crimes have all too often been mistreated by their governments.

Now the *Convention for the Suppression of the Financing of Terrorism* provides some of the needed protection. Article 15 reads:

> Nothing in this Convention shall be interpreted as imposing an obligation to extradite or to afford mutual legal assistance, if the requested State Party has substantial grounds for believing that the request for extradition for offenses set forth in article 2 or for mutual legal assistance with respect to such offenses has been made for the purpose of prosecuting or punishing a person on account of that person's race, religion, nationality, ethnic origin or political opinion or that compliance with the request would cause prejudice to that person's position for any of these reasons (United Nations 1999, Article 9.1).

Thus this convention replaces the traditional political offenses exception to extradition with a very different exception designed to serve the same purpose. On the whole, one should conclude that the various conventions against terrorism do not violate the moral limits on justified treaties in any serious manner.

4.3 Security Council Resolutions

Although international conventions impose legal obligations only upon state parties, those nation states that have agreed to them, the Security Council has the power to impose obligations upon all the members of the United Nations with or without their consent. Article 39 of Chapter VII of the *Charter of the United Nations* reads:

> The Security Council shall determine the existence of any threat to the peace, breach of the peace, or act of aggression and shall make recommendations, or decide what measures shall be taken in accordance with Articles 41 and 42, to maintain or restore international peace and security (United Nations 1945).

Article 41 authorizes the Security Council to "decide what measures not involving the use of armed force are to be employed," and Article 42 provides that "it may take such action by air, sea, or land forces as may be necessary to maintain or restore international peace and security." The Security Council has exercised its authority under each of these articles to suppress international terrorism.

In its Resolution 748 (1992), the Security Council imposed sanctions against Libya because it had not provided a full and effective response to previous requests to identify and extradite those responsible for the destruction of Pan Am flight 103 and the UTA flight 772. Among other actions, it decided that all states shall:

> 4(a) Deny permission to any aircraft to take off from, land in or overfly their territory if it is destined to land in or has taken off from the territory of Libya....4(b) Prohibit, by their nationals or from their territory, the supply of any aircraft or aircraft components to Libya....
> 6(a) Significantly reduce the number and level of the staff at Libyan diplomatic missions and consular posts and restrict or control the movement within their territory of all such staff who remain....
> 6(b) Prevent the operation of all Libyan Arab Airlines offices... (Security Council 1992, p. 55).

Here is a forceful international response to terrorism that does not involve the use of armed force.

Again Security Council Resolution 1333 (2000) imposed sanctions against the Taliban for the sheltering and training of terrorists and planning terrorist acts within Afghanistan. Examples are its decisions that all States shall:

> 5(a) Prevent the direct or indirect supply, sale and transfer to the territory of Afghanistan under Taliban control...by their nationals or from their territories, or using their flag vessels or aircraft, of arms and related material of all types including weapons and ammunition, military vehicles and equipment, paramilitary equipment, and spare parts for the aforementioned.8(a) Close immediately and completely all Taliban offices in their territories.
> 8(b) Close immediately all offices of Ariana Afghan Airlines in their territories.
> 8(c) Freeze without delay funds and other financial assets of Usama bin Laden and individuals and entities associated with him as designated by the Committee, including those in the Al-Qaida organization... (Security Council 2000, p. 274).

The Security Council justified its imposition of sanctions against Libya and the Taliban as measures both to restore or secure peace and to protect human rights. These are morally relevant considerations with considerable justificatory force.

However, human rights also constitute a moral limit on the justified imposition of sanctions. As the UN Secretary-General Boutros Boutros Ghali observed:

> Sanctions, as is generally recognized, are a blunt instrument. They raise the ethical question of whether suffering inflicted on vulnerable groups in the target country is a legitimate means of exerting pressure on political leaders whose behavior is unlikely to be affected by the plight of their subjects. Sanctions always have unintended or unwanted effects (Boutros Ghali 1995, p. 70).

The Security Council recognized this moral limit in the preface to Resolution 1333:

> Reaffirming the necessity for sanctions to contain adequate and effective exemptions to avoid adverse humanitarian consequences on the people of Afghanistan, and that they be structured in a way that will not impede, thwart or delay the work of international humanitarian assistance organizations or governmental relief agencies providing humanitarian assistance to the civilian population in the country (Security Council 2000, p. 274).

Nevertheless, when it decided in 8(c) that all States shall freeze the funds and other financial assets of Usama bin Laden and individuals and entities associated with him as designated by the Al-Qaida Sanctions Committee and requested the Committee to maintain an updated list of such individuals and entities, it failed to include any provisions regarding due process to protect the human right to property of those listed. And subsequently when the list was used to deny individuals the right to travel internationally, their human right to liberty was rendered insecure. As an armchair moral philosopher, I lack the empirical data to judge whether on balance this omission rendered these responses to terrorism unjustified. But I can and do insist that humanitarian considerations, and more broadly the human rights of those affected, limit the moral justification of any sanctions against terrorism.

When the sanctions imposed against the Taliban proved inadequate to suppress terrorism, the Security Council, acting on the authority of Article 42 of the *Charter of the United Nations*, took military action. Security Council Resolution 1386 (2001b) reads in part:

> The Security Council,
>
> 1. *Authorizes*, as envisaged in annex 1 to the Bonn Agreement, the establishment for six months of an International Security Assistance Force to assist the Afghan Interim Authority in the maintenance of security in Kabul and its surrounding area, so that the Afghan Interim Authority as well as the personnel of the United Nations can operate in a secure environment;
> 2. *Calls upon* Member States to contribute personnel, equipment and other resources to the International Security Assistance Force, and invites those Member States to inform the leadership of the Force and the Security Council;
> 3. *Authorizes* the Member States participating in the International Security Assistance Force to take all necessary measures to fulfil its mandate; ... (Security Council 2001b, p. 268).

This resolution authorizing the use of military force may well have been morally justified as a means of meeting the threat to international peace posed by terrorism and as a way of preventing the Taliban from continuing its violation of the human rights of the population of Afghanistan.

However because military action inevitably causes serious harm and often violates the human rights to property, personal security and even life of innocent victims, its justification is limited by the moral principles of necessity and proportionality. The use of military force is not justified when it is not necessary, when there is some less harmful means of promoting its justificatory purpose. The Security Council explicitly recognized this limitation. In its preface to Resolution 1386, it explains that it is taking this action because "the situation in Afghanistan still constitutes a threat to international peace and security" (Security Council 2001b, p. 268). The word "still" reminds the reader that this action is being taken only after the imposition of sanctions had proven insufficient. And in its operative provisions, it authorized the participating Member States to take only "all necessary measures to fulfil its mandate." Even when military action is necessary, it is fully justified only when it is proportionate. That is, the harm it causes and its violation of human rights must not exceed the seriousness of the evils it is intended to prevent. This moral limit may be recognized in the very limited mandate given to the International Security Assistance Force, only "to assist the Afghan Interim Authority in the maintenance of security in Kabul and its surrounding area..." (Security Council 2001b, p. 268). And presumably the mandate "to assist" the Afghan Interim Authority respects the sovereignty of Afghanistan as well as is possible under the circumstances. Whether the military operations carried out under color of Security Council authorization have actually respected these moral limits is probably controversial.

Increasingly concerned by the possibility that terrorists might obtain and use weapons of mass destruction, the Security Council adopted Resolution 1540 (2004). Its operative paragraphs begin:

> *Acting* under Chapter VII of the Charter of the United Nations,
>
> 1. *Decides that* all States shall refrain from providing any form of support to non-state actors that attempt to develop, acquire, manufacture, possess, transport, transfer or use nuclear, chemical or biological weapons and their means of discovery;
> 2. *Decides also* that all States, in accordance with their national procedures, shall adopt and enforce appropriate effective laws which prohibit any non-State actor to manufacture, acquire, possess, develop, transport, transfer or use nuclear, chemical or biological weapons and their means of delivery, in particular for terrorist purposes, as well as attempts to engage in any of the foregoing activities, participate in them as an accomplice, assist or finance them;
> 3. *Decides also* that all States shall take and enforce effective measures to establish domestic controls to prevent the proliferation of nuclear, chemical, or biological weapons and their means of delivery, including by establishing appropriate controls over related materials... (Security Council 2004, p. 544).

These provisions reflect, but go beyond, a number of earlier United Nations conventions.

> It was for this reason that the Security Council included paragraph 5 providing that:... none of the obligations set forth in this resolution shall be interpreted so as to conflict with or alter the rights and obligations of State Parties to the Nuclear Non-Proliferation Treaty, the Chemical Weapons Convention and the Biological and Toxic Weapons Convention or alter the responsibilities of the International Atomic Energy Agency or the Organization for the Prohibition of Chemical Weapons... (Security Council 2004, p. 545).

Why, then, did the Security Council adopt Resolution 1540 (2004)? Primarily because it imposes obligations to prevent terrorists from obtaining and using weapons of mass destruction upon all nation states, not only those that have agreed to the related treaties. However, it does this in a manner that respects the national sovereignty of those states that have agreed or in the future will agree to these related conventions. On the whole, then, Security Council has certainly endeavored to limit its imposition of sanctions and other legal obligations as well as the authorization of military action by the limiting moral considerations.

4.4 Criminalization

The United Nations (1963) has sponsored a number of international treaties that have made specified acts often committed by terrorists criminal offenses under international law. These include the Convention on Offences and Certain Other Acts Committed on Board Aircraft, the 1979 International Convention against the Taking of Hostages, the 1997 International Convention for the Suppression of Terrorist Bombings and the 1999 International Convention for the Suppression of the Financing of Terrorism. However, repeated efforts to draft a general international convention against terrorism that would be ratified by any significant number of nation states have failed. Hence, terrorism as such is not a criminal offense under international treaty law.

However, it can be argued that the international community is in the process of, and may even have completed the process of, criminalizing terrorism under international customary law. Article 38.1(b) of the Statute of the International Court of Justice defines an international custom as "a general practice accepted as law." Antonio Cassese describes the evidence of a general practice as follows:

> The requisite practice (*usus*) lies in, or results from, the converging adoption of national laws, the handing down of judgments by national courts, the passing of UN GA resolutions, as well as the ratification of international conventions by a great number of states (such ratifications evincing the attitude of states on the matter) (Cassese 2008, p.163).

Because almost all members of the United Nations have taken such actions, it would appear that this element in an international custom making terrorism as such a crime has come into existence.

On the other hand, some jurists would deny that most nation states have taken these actions because they believe that they are required by international law. Cassese also reports that:

> Interminable polemical arguments have been exchanged between states since the 1970 s over what should be meant by terrorism. The bone of contention is twofold: could 'freedom fighters' engaged in national liberation movements be classified as terrorists? Should the working out of international rules on terrorism be made contingent upon delving into the root causes of this phenomenon? Many states have asserted that as long as no agreement is reached on these two contentious issues, no consent could evolve on the very notion of terrorism either (Cassese 2008, pp. 162–163).

Because these disagreements continue, one may doubt that the second element required for any international custom, *opinio juris*, now exists.

Nevertheless, there is considerable evidence that the international community does regard terrorism as such criminal. Although the General Assembly in its Resolution 3034 (1972) merely expressed its "*deep concern* over increasing acts of violence which endanger or take innocent human lives or jeopardize fundamental freedoms," it later condemned terrorism as such. Subsequently the first operative provision of its Resolution 40/61 (1985) affirms that the General Assembly: "*Unequivocally condemns*, as criminal, all acts, methods and practices of terrorism whatever and by whomever committed, including those which jeopardize friendly relations among States and their security." And in its Resolution 49/60 (1994) and again in its Resolution 53/08 (1999) it condemn all acts of terrorism as criminal. Notice that these resolutions condemn all acts of terrorism, not merely specific forms of terrorism, and that they condemn them as criminal. Similarly, the second paragraph of the Security Council Resolution 1617 (2005) reads in part:

> *Reaffirming* that terrorism in all its forms and manifestations constitutes one of the most serious threats to peace and security and that any acts of terrorism are criminal and unjustifiable regardless of their motivations, whenever and by whomsoever committed... (*Security* Council 2005, p. 410).

Thus, it would appear that the *opinio juris* required for the existence of the criminalization of terrorism in international law is at least emerging and may already have been achieved.

To be sure, the *Rome Statute of the International Criminal Court* does not list terrorism as one of the crimes over which the court has jurisdiction. Robert Arnold suggests that a major reason for this omission is that since there is no universally accepted definition yet, its inclusion may have thrown the court into major political debates, thereby jeopardizing its acceptance and functioning (Arnold 2004, p. 335). But Cassese argues that there is a generally agreed definition of terrorism implicit in the evidences of an international custom criminalizing it. (Cassese 2008, pp. 164–165). If this is so, then any individual who commits an act of terrorism could be prosecuted in the judicial system of any nation state. What remains lacking may be an international court with general jurisdiction over acts of terrorism. Although this may prove a serious problem in enforcing the criminalization of terrorism in international law, it does not undermine the conclusion that both elements required for the existence of an international custom, a general practice and *opinio juris*, really do exist.

Leaving to jurists the question of whether the process of criminalizing terrorism in international law has been completed, what could morally justify this response of the international community? In the prefatory paragraphs of its Resolution 40/61, the General Assembly justifies its condemnation of terrorism as criminal thus:

> *Deeply concerned* about the world-wide escalation of acts of terrorism in all its forms, which endanger or take innocent human lives, jeopardize fundamental freedoms and seriously impair the dignity of human beings,...*Expressing its concern* that in recent years terrorism has taken on forms that have an increasingly deleterious effect on international relations, which may jeopardize the very territorial integrity and security of States,... (General Assembly 1985, p. 1168).

These words suggest four moral reasons to criminalize terrorism. It inflicts serious harms on innocent persons, jeopardizes their human rights, undermines friendly relations among nation states even threatening international peace, and often violates the sovereignty of nation states. Each of these is a relevant and important moral concern, and together they provide a very strong prima facie justification for criminalizing terrorism in international law.

At the same time, there are moral limits to the criminalization of terrorism that the international community ought to respect. Although the serious harms that terrorism causes constitute a moral reason to make it a crime in international law, the enforcement of any prohibition of terrorism will impose the harms of at least fines or loss of liberty on those punished for this offense as well as costs upon the international legal system. These harms require that terrorism be criminalized only when it cannot be greatly reduced or eliminated by any less harmful measures. The General Assembly respected this limit, for it began with measures to prevent terrorism by eliminating its causes in Resolution 3034 (1972) and only in Resolution 49/60 (1995), when these measures had failed, did it condemn it as a crime and require states to take measures to eliminate terrorism. Similarly, the Security Council began by imposing sanctions against Libya in its Resolution 748 (1992) and against Sudan in Resolution 1269 (1999) but did not decide until Resolution 1373 (2001a) that all states shall criminalize the financing of terrorism.

Again, although the fact that terrorism violates the human rights of innocent victims justifies its criminalization, human rights also limit this justification. The General Assembly recognized this dual role of human rights in Resolution 59/191 (2004) entitled "Protection of human rights and fundamental freedoms while countering terrorism." In particular, any prohibition of terrorism as a crime must define terrorism in terms determinate enough to ensure that the implementation of international law will not violate the human rights against discrimination or to the equal protection of the law. When a crime is defined in vague terms, those who enforce the law have wide discretion as to whom to punish. As a consequence, they all too often unfairly single out those against whom they are prejudiced for punishment and arbitrarily deprive them, but not others who are similarly situated, of property or liberty, sometimes even life. Because the United Nations has been unable to formulate any generally accepted definition of terrorism, it has sponsored no general convention against terrorism. However, Antonio Cassese argues that a generally agreed definition of terrorism has been achieved in customary international law (Cassese 2008, pp. 164–169). If this is true and if this definition can be formulated in relatively precise terms, then the criminalization of terrorism in international law may well be morally justified.

However, it is essential that this is a definition of only international terrorism so that it does not apply to domestic terrorism. Hence, Cassese explains: "Furthermore, the conduct must be *transnational* in nature; that is, not limited to the territory of one state with no foreign elements or links whatsoever (in which case it would exclusively fall under the domestic criminal system of that state)" (Cassese 2008, p. 166). This limitation is morally required because the principle of nonintervention in the domestic affairs of any nation state is morally justified as a protection of the right to sovereignty of each nation state. And this is in turn morally justified in order that each state can effectively fulfil its moral duties to protect its residents from serious harms or the violation of their human rights.

Although the right to self-determination is not a human right, because it is a group right of peoples rather than a right of individual human beings, it probably imposes another moral limit on the justified criminalization of terrorism (United Nations 1966a, b, Article 1). The international community ought not to criminalize as terrorism the violent actions of any people legitimately fighting for national liberation or against domination by an alien power. However, precisely how to formulate this exception remains an unsolved problem. Jurists and moral philosophers, not to mention politicians, disagree as to when the violent actions of individuals claiming to be acting on behalf of a people are properly ascribed to a people and when violent tactics in a just cause exceed the limits of proportionality. It is also unclear how much weight to give to any moral right to self-determination. Still, some exception to permit the legitimate exercise of the right to self-determination ought to be included in any criminalization of international terrorism.

4.5 Supervision

The United Nations is, as its name implies, an international organization of sovereign nation states. It is not a super-state or global government. It has no legislature and no international police force and no standing army, navy or air force. Hence, the resolutions of its General Assembly and Security Council and the international treaties it sponsors must be enforced primarily by the member nation states themselves. However, it has recognized both that many states lack the ability to counter terrorism effectively and that most states are tempted to adopt counter-terrorism measures that violate human rights. Accordingly, it has created a number of bodies to supervise the ways in which nation states respond to terrorism.

The first of these was the United Nations Commission on Human Rights, now replaced by the Human Rights Council. From its creation in 1946 until 1967, its policy was to promote human rights while strictly respecting national sovereignty. Only in 1967 did it adopt an interventionist policy of investigating and reporting on human rights violations.

The Commission has adopted a number of resolutions concerning terrorism. A representative sample is its Human Rights Resolution 2002/35 in response to "the horrific events of 11 September 2001 in the United States of America." Its operative paragraphs include the following:

1. *Reiterates its unequivocal condemnation* of all acts, methods and practices of terrorism, regardless of their motivation, in all their forms and manifestations, wherever, whenever and by whomever committed, as acts aimed at the destruction of human rights, fundamental freedoms and democracy, threatening the territorial integrity and security of States, destabilizing legitimately constituted Governments, undermining pluralistic civil society and the rule of law and having adverse consequences for the economic and social development of the State; ...

> 5. Urges States to fulfill their obligations under the Charter of the United Nations in strict conformity with international law, including human rights standards and obligations and international humanitarian law, to prevent, combat and eliminate terrorism in all its forms and manifestations, wherever, whenever and by whomever committed, and calls upon States to strengthen, where appropriate, their legislation to combat terrorism in all its forms and manifestations (Commission on Human Rights 2002, p. 3).

Like many other resolutions of United Nations bodies, the Commission here asserts both that international terrorism violates human rights and that counter-terrorism measures must respect them.

In its earlier Resolution 1999/27 and 2000/30, the Commission on Human Rights requested its Special Rapporteur to give attention to a number of questions including its concern that counter-terrorism action may not fully comply with international human rights standards. Among the most relevant paragraphs of the ensuing report are the following:

> 107. When terrorist acts or threats of terrorism by non-State actors threaten the lives and safety of persons under a State's jurisdiction, it is the responsibility and the duty of the State to protect those persons....110. In this context, the rights to freedom of speech, association, belief, religion and movement, and the rights of refugees are particularly vulnerable to undue suspension in the guise of anti-terrorism measures. This may sometimes occur when individuals or groups in a State express support for a political position that is in opposition to the government's position but conforms with that espoused by a group labeled as terrorist.
> 115. Some States have provisions that affect the actual judicial proceedings. For example, persons accused of terrorist acts may be limited in the number of witnesses that may be called, or may even be denied any witnesses at all. This can seriously impair any attempt by a defendant to prove that he or she has no association with a particular group considered to be terrorist, or had nothing to do with a particular act. This could be of great importance if the person is charged not with a terrorist act directly but under group liability statutes.
> 117. Judicial process rights may be especially at risk when a State uses group liability or conspiracy laws against alleged members of groups labeled as terrorist. For example, a person who may have once distributed literature relating to the same goal as an alleged terrorist group could be charged with aiding and abetting terrorism and could be charged with any acts proved to have been carried out by the group—acts of which a defendant has no involvement or even awareness... (Commission on Human Rights 2001, pp. 29–31).

The subsequent publication of this report might have been helpful in reminding nation state of some of the ways in which their responses to terrorism too often fail to respect the moral limits imposed by human rights. However, the only procedure available for the Commission to hold states responsible for any violation of international human rights is a system requiring nation states to submit periodic human rights reports. These are typically very general and very little pressure is exerted by the Commission to rectify any deficiencies identified.

A second international body that supervises the ways in which nation states respond to terrorism is the United Nations Human Rights Committee. This committee was created pursuant to Article 28 of the *International Covenant on Civil and Political Rights*. It monitors the ways in which nation states protect or fail to protect human rights in three ways. It studies and comments upon reports that each state party is required to submit every five years. It receives and considers communications by one state party that claim that another state party is not fulfilling its obligations under the Covenant. And under the First Optional Protocol, it judges the merits of complaints submitted by individuals who allege violations of their civil or political human rights.

For obvious reasons, the Human Rights Committee has not been very effective in preventing nation states from adopting counter-terrorism measures that threaten or infringe human rights. State parties tend to sanitize their reports to omit any measures that might elicit criticism from the Committee. Nation states are seldom in a position to complain that another state has violated the human rights of its nationals because this is possible only when the state complained against has recognized the competence of the Committee to consider communications to this effect. And very few individuals, other than Hermanos Gómez Paquiyauri, have submitted complaints concerning counter-terrorism measures. Thus, the *Follow-up Progress Report of the Human Rights Committee on Individual Communications* of its 2010 session mentions no cases concerning terrorism. However, the Committee has made trenchant criticisms of counter-terrorism measures in several of its comments on state reports and in at least two of its General Comments. But, unlike the Security Council, it has no power to impose sanctions against any state that continues to violate the human rights of persons under its jurisdiction.

A third international body that supervises state responses to terrorism is the Counter-Terrorism Committee created by the Security Council in its Resolution 1373 of 2001. Article 6 reads:

> Decides to establish, in accordance with rule 28 of its provisional rules of procedure, a Committee of the Security Council, consisting of all the members of the Council, to monitor implementation of this resolution, with the assistance of appropriate expertise, and calls upon all States to report to the Committee, no later than 90 days from the date of the adoption of this resolution and thereafter according to a timetable to be prepared by the Committee, on the steps they have taken to implement this resolution (Security Council 2001a, p. 63).

Notice that the Committee is charged with monitoring the implementation of Resolution 1373 and that the primary purpose of this resolution is to combat international terrorism by imposing upon all nation states a wide variety of obligations to create and maintain counter-terrorism measures. Probably for this reason, and also to ensure the cooperation of reporting states, Ambassador Greenstock, the first Chairman of the Committee, decided that it was not a sanctions committee, nor was its task to prosecute or condemn states. Accordingly, it has operated primarily to urge nation states to adopt more effective counter-terrorism measures and to assist them in doing so. It has not, and presumably will not in the future, take any active role in ensuring that these measures respect the human rights of those affected. To my mind, it has gone too far in limiting its supervision out of a respect for the sovereignty of nation states.

Fourth, there is no global international court of human rights to supervise the counter-terrorism measures of nation states as effectively as the European Court of Human Rights or the Inter-American Court of Human Rights. Individual persons lack standing to petition the International Court of Justice regarding alleged violations of their human rights and terrorist acts are not specifically included in the categories of acts over which the International Criminal Court has jurisdiction.

However, there is at least one judgment of the International Court of Justice (2004) that does concern a state response to terrorism. It is the Israel Wall (Advisory Opinion) of 9 July 2004. This is in reply to a request of the United Nations General Assembly that the Court advise it of the legal consequences of the construction of a wall in the occupied Palestinian territory. After rejecting the grounds on which Israel claimed that it lacked jurisdiction (paras. 13–42), the International Court of Justice reasoned that Israel had violated international law in building the wall to protect its citizens from terrorist attacks. Specifically, it explained how building the wall violated the principle prohibiting the acquisition of territory by force and interfered with the right of self-determination of the Palestinian people. It also violated international humanitarian law, especially the Fourth Geneva Convention. Finally, construction of the wall impeded the exercise of a number of human rights including the rights to liberty of movement, to work, to health, to education, and to an adequate standard of living (paras. 114–142). Whatever the legal merits of this decision, it seems a morally justified exercise of the court's power to supervise state responses to terrorism.

4.6 Conclusion

During the past few decades, terrorism has become more frequent, more destructive and more international. This explains why the international community has responded to terrorism in a number of increasingly forceful ways. The General Assembly began with measures to prevent international terrorism, primarily by removing its causes, and moved on to measures to eliminate terrorism by urging nation states to enact and enforce laws against terrorist acts. The United Nations sponsored a series of international conventions criminalizing specific kinds of acts often committed by terrorists, such as high-jacking airplanes or taking hostages, but has not succeeded in its efforts to draft an acceptable general convention against terrorism as such. The Security Council first imposed sanctions against states that failed to cooperate in the prosecution and punishment of terrorists and later authorized the use of armed force against the Taliban. A general international custom prohibiting terrorism as such has been developing and may even have become a fully valid principle in international law. Finally, a number of United Nations bodies have supervised the responses of nation states to the threat of terrorism. The international community has justified its responses as actions necessary to protect the human rights of potential victims of terrorism and of those affected by state responses to terrorism and as a means to preserve international peace and promote friendly relations among nation states. These are clearly relevant considerations with considerable moral weight.

On the other hand, there are significant moral reasons that limit the justification of any response to terrorism that the international community might take. The external sovereignty of nation states requires that the international community criminalize or take other forceful measures against terrorism only when it is international in nature, only when it involves more than one nation state or nationals of more than one state. And measures to suppress terrorism must respect the human rights of all those affected by these measures. For example, the confiscation of funds that might be used to finance terrorism must not violate the property rights of innocent individuals and those detained as terrorists must be accorded due process if prosecuted and not subjected to torture when interrogated. Finally, international terrorism should be defined in such a way that it does not prohibit the violent actions of those legitimately exercising their group right to self-determination in their struggle for national liberation or against alien domination. To date, the international community has for the most part respected reasonably well these moral limits in its responses to terrorism.

References

Arnold R (2004) The ICC as an instrument for repressing terrorism. Transnational Publishers, Ardsley

Boutros Ghali B (1995) Supplement to an agenda for peace. In: Yearbook of the United Nations 1995. New York, pp 175–177

Cassese A (2008) International criminal law, 2nd edn. Oxford University Press, Oxford

Commission on Human Rights (2001) The impact of terrorism on human rights. Available at E/CN.4/Sub.2/2001/31, pp 28–33

Commission on Human Rights (2002) Resolution 2002/35. Terrorism and human rights. Available at FTR 2002/UN Commission

General Assembly (1948) Universal declaration of human rights. In: Yearbook of the United Nations 1948–1949. Columbia University Press, New York, pp 535–537, 1950

General Assembly (1960). Declaration on granting independence to colonial countries and peoples. In: Yearbook of the United Nations 1960. Columbia University Press, New York, pp 49–50

General Assembly (1970) Resolution 2625(XXV). Declaration on principles of international law concerning friendly relations and co-operation among states in accordance with the Charter of the United Nations. In: Yearbook of the United Nations 1970, New York, pp 788–792

General Assembly (1972) Resolution 3034. Measures to prevent international terrorism. In: Yearbook of the United Nations 1972. New York, pp 649–657

General Assembly (1985) Resolution 40/61 measures to prevent international terrorism. In: Yearbook of the United Nations 1985. New York, pp 1167–1168

General Assembly (1994) Resolution 49/60. Measures to eliminate international terrorism. In: Yearbook of the United Nations 1994. New York, pp 1293–1295

General Assembly (1999). Resolution 53/108. In: Yearbook of the United Nations 1999. New York, 2001

General Assembly (2004) Resolution 59/191. Protection of human rights and fundamental freedoms while countering terrorism. In: Yearbook of the United Nations 2004. New York, pp 741–744, 2006

Human Rights Committee (1984) General comment 12. Available at CCPR Genetal Comment No. 12

International Court of Justice (1966) South West Africa cases (Second Phase). In: International Court of Justice Reports 1966, p 6

International Court of Justice (1970) Barcelona Light and Power Company, limited, case, judgment. In: International Court of Justice Reports 1970, p 3

International Court of Justice (2004) Legal consequences of the construction of a wall in the occupied Palestinian territory (advisory opinion). In: International Court of Justice Reports 2004, p 136

International Law Commission (1966). In: Yearbook of the International law Commission, 1966, vol II. New York, pp 247–249

Petersen AC (1992) Extradition and the political offense exception in the suppression of terrorism. Indiana L J 67:767–796

Security Council (1992) Resolution 748. In: Yearbook of the United Nations 1992, New York, pp 55–56

Security Council (1999) Resolution 1269. In: Yearbook of the United Nations 1999. New York, pp 1240–1241

Security Council (2000) Resolutions 1333. In: Yearbook of the United Nations 2000. New York, pp 273–276

Security Council (2001a) Resolution 1373. In: Yearbook of the United Nations 2001. New York, pp 61–63

Security Council (2001b) Resolution 1386. In: Yearbook of the United Nations 2001. New York, pp 267–268

Security Council (2003) Resolution 1456. In: Yearbook of the United Nations 2003, pp 63–65. United Nations, pp 267–268

Security Council (2004) Resolution 1540. In: Yearbook of the United Nations 2004. New York, pp 544–545

Security Council (2005) Resolution 1617. In: Yearbook of the United Nations 2005. New York, pp 410–413

United Nations (1945) Charter of the United Nations. 1 UNTS (XVI)

United Nations (1963). 704 UNTS 219

United Nations (1966a) International covenant on civil and political rights. 999UNTS 171

United Nations (1966b) International convention on the elimination of all forms of racial discrimination. 660 UNTS 195

United Nations (1969) Vienna convention on the Law of Treaties. 1155 UNTS 331

United Nations (1972) Questions relating to international terrorism. In: Yearbook of the United Nations 1972. New York, pp 639–650

United Nations (1979) Convention against the taking of hostages. 1316 UNTS 205

United Nations (1999) Convention for the suppression of the financing of terrorism. 2178 UNTS 197

United Nations (2005) International convention for the suppression of acts of nuclear terrorism. In: Yearbook of the United Nations 2005. New York, pp 1411–1416

Chapter 5
State Responses

Abstract Measures of counterterrorism by nation states can be justified as necessary to self-defense, to the preservation of national sovereignty, and to the protection of its citizens from serious harm or the violation of their human rights. However, there are also moral limits to state responses. Surveillance should respect the human right to privacy. Detention is limited by the human right to liberty. Interrogation ought not to include torture as a means of exacting information. Trials should be conducted with adequate due process of law. Targeted killing of terrorist leaders in justified only when it is absolutely necessary to prevent an imminent attack and there is strong reason to believe that it will be effective. Intrusion into or invasion of another nation state can be justified only when it is necessary to defend the vital interests of a state or protect its citizens from very serious violations of their human rights. In addition, states have a moral obligation to alleviate the injustices that often generate terrorism. What matters for the justification of each state response is not some overall balancing of national security against moral rights, but the contribution of each response to the prevention of harm and the protection of rights weighed against the relevant moral limits on this sort of response.

There are many kinds of terrorism, but the most important and most controversial are large scale and ongoing. These have inflicted grievous harm on many human beings and threaten to continue to do so in the future. They are normally directed against one or more nation states or against some significant portion of their nationals. The attacks of al Queda against the United States may spring first to mind, but these are not definitive. Other examples are the terrorist campaigns of the Irish Republican Army against the United Kingdom, the Tamil Tigers against the government of Bangladesh, Hamas against Israel, and Sunni and Shi'a Muslims against each other within Iraq.

Presumably nation states are morally justified in using any means, including violent police and even military action, necessary to identify the terrorists and prevent them from inflicting serious harms and violating human rights in the future. If the terrorism is directed against a state as such, its responses could be justified by its right of self-defense, the necessity of defending its very existence or perhaps its vital interests. If the terrorism is intended to coerce the state into abandoning or changing some important policy, it could appeal to its right to external sovereignty,

C. Wellman, *Terrorism and Counterterrorism*, SpringerBriefs in Law 9,
DOI: 10.1007/978-94-007-6007-3_5, © The Author(s) 2013

its right that other states or groups not interfere in its domestic affairs. If the terrorism is directed against some segment of its population, state responses could be justified by its right, even its duty, to prevent serious harm to its citizens and to protect their human rights. Often more than one justification will be applicable so that the primary justification will be reinforced by others.

The most common justification of counterterrorism measures is that they increase the security of the state and its citizens, and the most common criticism is that they curtail the liberty of its citizens to an excessive degree. In any such debate, both sides agree that the moral assessment of any state response to terrorism requires primarily weighing the increase of security against the loss of liberty. Eric A. Posner and Adrian Vermeule explain this assumption very clearly.

> We assume that there is a basic tradeoff between security and liberty. Both are valuable goods that contribute to social welfare, so neither good can simply be maximized without regard for the other….The problem from the social point of view is one of optimization: it is to choose the point along the frontier that maximizes the join benefits of security and liberty (Posner and Vermeule 2006, p. 1098).

However, not everyone shares this assumption.

Laura K. Donohue cautions that this dominant paradigm of a tradeoff between security and freedom is perilous:

> But in the rush to pass new measures, legislators rarely incorporate sufficient oversight authorities. New powers end up being applied to nonterrorists—often becoming part of ordinary criminal law. And temporary provisions rarely remain so—instead, they become a baseline on which future measures are built. At each point at which the legislature would otherwise be expected to push back—at the introduction of the measures, at the renewal of the temporary provisions, and in the exercise of oversight—its ability to do so is limited. The judiciary's role, too, is restricted: constitutional structure and cultural norms narrow the court's ability to check the executive at all but the margins (Donohue 2008, p. 2).

Donohue goes on to argue that:

> Some rights are fundamental to liberal democracy and cannot be relinquished. Setting such rights to one side, the security or freedom framework fails to capture the most important characteristic of counterterrorist law: it increase executive power, both in absolute and relative terms, and, in so doing, alters the relationships among the branches of government with implications well beyond the state's ability to respond to terrorism. But this is not the only omission. Missing, too, are the broad social, political, and economic effects of counterterrorism. The dichotomy also glosses over the complex nature of both security and freedom. The resulting danger is that the true cost of the new powers goes uncalculated—to the detriment of the state (Donohue 2008, p. 3).

Donohue denotes an entire book to the explanation of these costs.

Jeremy Waldron also argues for extreme caution when assessing state responses to terrorism by balancing security against liberty. In particular, he advances four objections to the balancing approach.

(i) *Objections to consequentialism.* Talk of balance—particularly talk of changes in the balance as circumstances and consequences change—may not be appropriate in the realm of civil liberties. Civil liberties are associated with rights, and rights-discourse is often resolutely anti-consequentialist….

(ii) *Difficulties with distribution*. Though we talk of balancing our liberties against our security, we need to pay some attention to the fact that the real diminution in liberty may affect some people more than others….

(iii) *Unintended effects*. When liberty is conceived of as *negative* liberty, a reduction in liberty is achieved by enhancing the power of the state. This is done so that the enhanced power can be used to combat terrorism. But it would be na to assume that this is the only thing that power can be used for….

(iv) *Real versus symbolic consequences*. Though talk of adjusting the balance sounds like hard-headed consequentialism, it often turns out that those who advocate it have no idea what difference it will actually make to the terrorist threat… (Waldron 2010, pp. 35–36).

To my mind, these objections clearly demonstrate that the dichotomy of security versus liberty is inadequate for any moral assessment of state responses to terrorism.

How, then, should one judge the counterterrorism measures of nation states? I have suggested that state responses to terrorism are prima facie justified by one or more rights of any nation state. These are the right of self-defense, the right to external sovereignty, and its right to protect its citizens. What, then, limits the moral justification of counterterrorism measures? Waldron suggests a more adequate basis for the moral criticism of any excessive state response to terrorism.

> This is the proposition I want to examine: a change in the scale and nature of the harms that threaten us explains and justifies a change in our scheme of civil liberties; and that process is best understood in terms of 'striking a new balance between liberty and security' (Waldron 2010, pp. 21–22).

Thus, what limits the justification of counterterrorism measures is not the loss of liberty in some generic sense, but violation or diminution of one or more specific civil liberties.

Moreover, what we call "civil liberties" are heterogeneous and are not all liberties in any strict sense.

(a) In its most straightforward meaning, the phrase 'civil liberties' refers to certain freedoms understood as actions that individuals might wish to perform, which (it is thought) the state should not restrict….

(b) We also use the phrase 'civil liberties' sometimes to refer to more diffuse concerns about government power….For example, the government's ability to eavesdrop electronically on telephone conversations or e-mail as a civil liberty concern, even though the 'liberty' in question—sometimes referred to as 'privacy'—does not amount to very much more than the condition of not being subjected to this scrutiny.

(c) Sometimes 'civil liberties' refers to procedural rights and powers which we think individuals should have when the state detains them or brings charges against them or plans to punish them.

(d) 'Civil liberties' is also used to refer to certain protections individuals are supposed to have against certain abuses that might be inflicted on them—for example, beatings, degrading treatment, and torture (Waldron 2010, pp. 26–27).

I would add only that for the moral evaluation of state responses to terrorism, one must consider the moral rights, primarily human rights, that typically justify any set of legal civil rights. Let us, then, examine some of the most important state responses to terrorism on this basis.

5.1 Surveillance

If a nation state is to prevent future acts of terrorism, it will need to identify potential terrorists and learn of their plans in order to take effective measures to defeat them. This will require extensive and intensive surveillance. My *American Heritage Dictionary* defines "surveillance" as "Close observation of a person or group, especially one under suspicion." But in the sense in which that term is used in discussions of terrorism, this includes the collection, storage and analysis of information about persons or groups.

The most obvious moral limit on surveillance in this sense is its invasion of the right to privacy. After reminding the reader of the world described in the novel *Nineteen Eighty Four* where there is no personal privacy, Patricia Mell reports:

> Advances in computer and surveillance technology, as well as the growth of internet use, have combined to make the constant surveillance of Orwell's novel a possibility. Many street intersections sport video cameras in the attempt to monitor traffic violators. Thermal imaging and spy satellites make it possible to observe the interior happenings of the home. Telephone, e-mail, Internet activity, and all other manners of electronic communication can be monitored. Biometric methods can be used to identify and track the individual's movement in society. In addition, it has been suggested that a National Identification Card be instituted as a means of monitoring travel patterns. Many of these methods can be used without an individual's knowledge. Today's technology has the potential to eliminate the areas in which an individual can legitimately declare privacy from the invasion of the government (Mell 2002, p. 376).

Any excessive attack on the informational privacy of individuals would clearly be morally objectionable.

Mell points to several provisions of the USA Patriot Act as especially dangerous to individual privacy.

> Current laws shape the parameters of the individual's sphere of privacy by declaring that certain information is not to be disclosed to third parties, including the government, except under specified extraordinary circumstances. The PATRIOT Act makes the disclosure of highly sensitive information routine between a large number of law enforcement agencies and other government personnel (Mell 2002, p. 393). Essentially, Section 216 allows the judge, operating under a relevance standard, to issue a blank warrant to a succession of communications carriers. This fails to meet the Fourth Amendment requirement of specifying the place to be searched. It also deprives the judge of the ability to monitor the extent to which governmental officials utilize the order to access information about internet communications (Mell 2002, p. 404).
>
> In its amendments to FISA, the PATRIOT Act abandons a long held taboo and extends domestic surveillance authority to the Central Intelligence Agency ("CIA"). This action eliminates a long recognized distinction between acceptable warrantless electronic surveillance performed in the name of national security and surveillance supported by probable cause necessary for the prosecution of ordinary criminal matters (Mell 2002, pp. 405–406).

Clearly these measures infringe upon the human right to privacy, but whether they do so in an unjustified manner remains debatable.

With the incorporation of the *European Convention for the Protection of Human Rights* into its domestic law, the British government decided to revise its legislation regarding surveillance.

> First, the state proposed to expand the interception of communications sent via post or public telecommunication systems to *all* communications by telecom operators or mail delivery services. Second, the state sought to relax warrant applications, tying them not to addresses, but to individuals, with a list of addresses and numbers attached and easily amendable by lower level officials. Third, to give the state flexibility to respond to emergencies, the authority to request wiretaps would be extended from the Senior Civil Service to the head of the agency involved. Fourth, the Labour government wanted to expand the length of time for which a warrant operated….Fifth, the government also proposed to expand its intercept authority to include private networks, with the aim of making it legal for businesses to record communications to create a paper trail of commercial transactions and business communications in both public and private sectors. Sixth, where previously communications data could be turned over voluntarily, the state wanted to compel targets to do so (Donohue 2008, p. 196).

These proposals were subsequently enacted in the 2000 Regulation of Investigatory Powers Act. Thus, individual privacy was threatened in the United Kingdom in ways similar to those adopted in the United States.

Article 12 of the *Universal Declaration of Human Rights* reads in part: "No one shall be subjected to arbitrary interference with his privacy, family, home or correspondence, nor to attacks upon his honour and reputation" (General Assembly 1948, p. 536). The human right affirmed here is primarily the right to informational privacy, not necessarily the right to make and act on private decisions first recognized by the United States Supreme court in *Griswold v. Connecticut* (Supreme Court 1965). This right to the privacy of personal information is recognized in international law in Article 17 of the *International Covenant on Civil and Political Rights* (United Nations 1966b) and in a wide variety of regional human rights documents. For present purposes I shall assume that this human right to privacy, and others to which I will refer later, have moral force because they are grounded upon strong moral reasons such as a more fundamental moral right to privacy or social justice or some other strong moral reason. To specify fully and clearly the moral grounds of these international human rights would require another and much longer explanation best reserved for another occasion (Wellman 2011, pp. 85–100).

No one imagines that the human right to privacy is absolute, that it renders even the slightest public surveillance morally wrong. For example, Article 8.2 of the *European Convention for the Protection of Human Rights and Freedoms* (Council of Europe 1950) prohibits any interference by a public authority with the human right to privacy *except* when necessary for a number of important state interests including national security, public safety, the prevention of disorder or crime and the protection of the rights of others. And most jurists and moral philosophers similarly maintain that some infringement of the human right to privacy is morally justified when this is necessary for some compelling state interest. Presumably many ways of collecting, storing and analyzing personal information can be justified by necessity.

However, the justification of surveillance by its necessity has its limits. When judging the adequacy of any alleged justification by necessity, one should ask three questions. (1) What kind of surveillance is necessary? No doubt a variety of measures to collect, store and analyze information about persons and groups is necessary to prevent terrorism. But this does not imply that any and all kinds if surveillance are justified. It may be necessary to intercept telephone messages or even e-mail, but not to gather information from third parties such as public libraries about the books checked out by their patrons or private banks about the purchases charged on their credit cards. The necessity of each kind of surveillance should be judged in its own terms. (2) For what purpose is this kind of surveillance necessary? There are several important state interests that might morally justify surveillance including national security or defense of the state, resistance against coercive interference with its external sovereignty and the protection of its residents from serious harm or the violation of their human rights. But these are distinct purposes, and a form of surveillance might be necessary for one of these but not for others. Until very recently, United States law recognized the relevance of different purposes by regulating domestic surveillance to combat crime by Title III of the *Omnibus Crime Control and Safe Streets Act* (United States 1968) but foreign surveillance by the *Foreign Intelligence Surveillance Act* (United States 1978) with less restrictive requirements for the collection and storing of intelligence presumably justified by the more urgent necessity of national security. (3) Is this kind of surveillance strictly necessary for its justifying purpose? Necessity exists only when there is no less objectionable means of achieving its purpose. If the state could defend its very existence or its nationals from terrorism by a different way of collecting, storing and analyzing information that would intrude less into personal privacy, then the more intrusive means are not morally justified by necessity.

Any infringement of the human right to privacy is morally justified only when it is necessary for some legitimate state interest. But how important must that interest be? Important enough, given the circumstances, to outweigh the right to privacy. Hence, the degree of invasion into individual privacy of the surveillance measures taken must be proportionate to and not exceed the urgency of the state interest. As Judge Wildhaber insisted in *Rotaru v. Romania*:

> States do not enjoy unlimited discretion to subject individuals to secret surveillance or a system of secret files. The interest of the State in protecting its national security must be balanced against the seriousness of the interference with an applicant's right to respect for his or her private life. Our Court has repeatedly stressed "the risk that a system of secret surveillance for the protection of national security poses of undermining or even destroying democracy on the ground of defending it".... (Wildhaber 2000, concurring opinion).

Accordingly, to assess any alleged justification of surveillance by its necessity, one must balance the state's need to conduct this surveillance in order to protect one or more legitimate state interests against the seriousness of the infringement of the right to privacy of all those affected by the surveillance at issue.

How should one weigh the state's need to conduct surveillance? Not by measuring it by some unit analogous to pounds and ounces, but by considering all the relevant factors. To assert that the state needs to conduct surveillance implies that if it does not do so, it be harmed. And this in turn implies that if it does not do so, then one of more of its interests will be negatively affected. Although any claim of necessity presupposes that the interest or interests at stake are important, the importance of these interests in general is not the relevant measure. To justify the necessity of any state actions of surveillance one must weigh the degree to which these specific actions will protect the presupposed state interests from damage.

Since any protection from harm is prospective preventive action, what must be weighed are not actual harms from past terrorism but potential harms from terrorism in the future. Hence, what one must weigh is the risk of harm, that is the seriousness of the possible harm and the probability that it will actually occur. And to complete the moral justification by an appeal to necessity, one must also explain how the surveillance measures at issue would in fact eliminate or at least reduce the risk of harm.

When one weighs potential harms, one would need to identify potential targets of terrorism, the weapons available to terrorists who might attack these targets, what kinds and amounts of damage the use of these weapons would inflict upon these targets, and how this damage would set back the state interest under threat by terrorism. Then to weigh the probability of these harms actually occurring, one should consider the number and abilities of the terrorists who might attack the state, the vulnerability of the prime targets should they attack, the weapons at their disposal, and their ability to deliver or use these weapons against these targets. Finally, to complete any case for the necessity of surveillance, one would need to explain precisely how the surveillance measures to be justified would eliminate or reduce the risks of terrorism against the state. This would require one to specify the kinds of information sought, how the surveillance measures would obtain it, and how it would be used to prevent attacks by terrorists or at least reduce the risks threatened by terrorism.

How should one weigh the seriousness of the infringement of the human right to privacy? The primary considerations will concern the potential harms to the right-holders, the individuals whose privacy will be invaded by the surveillance. One should explain how the infringement of the right to privacy might harm the right-holders. Examples come readily to mind. If the information is made public, it might damage their reputation. If disclosed to a public prosecutor, it might expose one at least to prosecution and perhaps criminal penalties. In any event, it shifts control over personal information from the right-holder to those who collect, store, analyze and disclose it. Hence, it endangers the right-holder in a way that she would not have been endangered if one's right of privacy were not infringed. Moreover, if people are aware of the surveillance measures, then additional harms are possible. They may wonder whether they are being subjected to surveillance and suffer anxiety over the possible consequences for them. If they fear any anticipated consequences, whether or not their fears are justified, they may modify or abandon projects and personal relationships that give value to their lives. They may even take evasive measures that impose personal or economic costs, for example, self-censorship of e-mail sent or refraining from discussing political issues even in the privacy of their homes or installing encryption devices in their computers.

Each of these kinds of harm might vary in amount from severe to minor. Hence, one should identify the factors that will increase or reduce them. Obviously the kind of information collected will be relevant. Evidence of criminal activity, especially any connection with terrorism, exposes one to great danger. Sexual orientation or interest in pornography could devastate one's reputation. Knowledge of the identity of one's friends or correspondents could threaten considerable or little harm depending upon the direction of the suspicions of those who collect the information and those to whom they disclose it. The degree of harm will depend not only on the kind of information collected, but also on how it is used. Potentially incriminating information might or might not be turned over to some public prosecutor. Knowledge of one's sexual orientation or one's membership in unpopular organizations may or may not be released to the public. Creating watch lists that will either impose extra security measures on those under suspicion or even prohibit their international travel altogether will at least impose inconvenience and may seriously handicap those whose vocations require them to travel extensively. If released to employers or potential employers, many sorts of personal information could result in losing one's position or threaten one's economic opportunity. Moreover, the more extensive the surveillance, the larger the number of individuals subjected to it, the greater will be the aggregate of harms produces.

Finally, one must assess the probability that each of these harms will occur. This will depend in large measure on how the intelligence is collected, stored, analyzed and disclosed. The more effective the techniques of surveillance are the greater will be the amount of potentially harmful information collected. The more secure the storage is the less opportunity there will be for misuse, either by those conducting surveillance or those able to gain unauthorized access to the information. The more widely sensitive information is disclosed the greater the probability of harm. However, the probability of harm can be reduced, perhaps significantly, by protections against misuse or leaks. These typically take the form of administrative regulations, statutes and judicial review that restrict the activities of those who conduct surveillance and impose penalties for any who violate these restrictions. Although the effectiveness of these and other forms of oversight is debatable, they should not be entirely discounted.

In addition to the potential harms to individual right-holders, one should consider the ways in which surveillance that infringes on privacy might harm important state interests. For example, it might cause individuals to withhold information in order to avoid becoming a suspect subject to more intensive surveillance. It might create a climate of suspicion of and alienation from the government that would reduce the ability of a wide variety of public officials to perform their duties. It might cause talented persons to reduce or avoid entirely forms of public service that they fear would expose them to greater surveillance.

This account of how one should weigh the state's need to conduct surveillance against the seriously of the infringement of the human right to privacy is surely not complete and probably not very perspicuous. But at least it indicates many of the kinds of facts that one should consider and how they are relevant in judging whether the means of surveillance are justified by their necessity in countering the threat of terrorism.

Discussions of the justification of surveillance to prevent or reduce the threat of terrorism often portray the moral issue in terms of the conflict between security and privacy, but the matter is not that simple. Human rights other than the right to privacy are often infringed by the collection, storage, analysis and disclosure of personal information. The potential harms that, as history shows, surveillance often inflicts upon innocent persons burdens their exercise of the human rights to freedom of speech, freedom of association and freedom of religion. In addition, because not all citizens will be equally subject to surveillance, it typically threatens the human right to equal protection of the law of members of those groups suspected, with or without reliable evidence, by the authorities. One should measure the seriousness of the infringement of these other human rights in the way, mutatis mutandis, described above. Although in most cases the seriousness of the infringements of these additional human rights will be less than that of the invasion of privacy, their combined seriousness will make it more difficult for necessity to justify surveillance. However, when the need for information to combat terrorism really is urgent, a responsibly targeted and rigorously supervised program of surveillance may well be morally justified by its necessity.

5.2 Detention

Another state response to terrorism is to detain several, often many, individuals in order to prevent further attacks by terrorists. The *Oxford English Dictionary* defines "detain" in the relevant sense as "Place or keep in confinement; keep as a prisoner, esp. without charge." Both the United Kingdom and the United States have responded to terrorism by detaining suspects, even indefinitely.

In 1922, the Civil Authorities (Special Powers) Act (SPA) gave the minister of Home Affairs for Northern Ireland the power "to take all such steps and issue such orders as may be necessary for preserving the peace and maintaining order." Under this statute, the government subsequently issued more than 100 regulations, one of which—Regulation 23—allowed the state to indefinitely imprison anyone suspected of acting, having acted, or "being about to act in a manner prejudicial to the preservation of peace and the maintenance of order" (Donohue 2008, pp. 36–37). The 2001 Anti-Terrorism, Crime, and Security Act (ATCSA) gave the British Secretary of State the authority to specifically designate ("certify") foreign individuals reasonably suspected of being a terrorist, and defined "terrorist" broadly, to include anyone with links to international terrorist organizations. Where either a point of law or practical considerations prevented deportation, the legislation provided for indefinite detention (Donohue 2008, p. 58).

On October 7, 2001, Bush announced that the US military had begun military strikes in Afghanistan. Six weeks later, on November 13, 2001, the President issues a Military Order stating that a "compelling government interest" required the indefinite detention of noncitizens. These noncitizens included not only members of al-Qaeda but also anyone who "has engaged in, aided or betted, or conspired to commit, acts of international terrorism, or acts of preparation therefore, that have caused, threaten to cause, or have as their aim to cause, injury to or adverse effects on the United States, its citizens, national security, foreign policy, or economy" and anyone who had knowingly harbored an international terrorist (Donohue 2008, pp. 71–72).

As one would expect, these measures have proved controversial.

Detention, whether by a nation state or a private kidnapper is prima facie immoral primarily because it infringes the human right to liberty. However, it is justified in any case where the importance of the state's need to detain some person outweighs the seriousness of the infringement of that individual's human right to privacy. The way to balance the necessity of detaining against the right to liberty is the same as the way to balance the necessity of state surveillance against the infringement of the human right to privacy. Hence, it would be redundant to describe it in any detail here. But one should recognize that the justification of detaining individuals requires a more compelling necessity than the justification of surveillance because the human right to liberty is typically much more important than the human right to privacy.

In writing the opinion of the court in *Hamdi v. Rumsfeld*, Justice O'Connor clearly recognized the great importance of the right to liberty to the individual when it is weighed against the state interest in detention:

> It is beyond question that substantial interests lie on both sides of the scale in this case. "Hamdi's private interest...affected by the official action"... is the most elemental of liberty interests—the interest in being free from physical detention by one's own government (Supreme Court 2004a, p. 529).

> Detention prevents the individual from engaging in any of the normal human activities that give meaning and value to one's life, participating in family life, interacting with friends and associates, earning a living or pursuing a career, and engaging in hobbies or one's favorite leisure activities.

And in his dissenting opinion, Justice Scalia quoted Blackstone regarding the value to society of the right to liberty:

> Of great importance to the public is the preservation of this personal liberty: for if once it were left in the power of any, the highest magistrate to imprison arbitrarily whomever he or his officers thought proper...there would soon be an end of all other rights and immunities....To bereave a man of life, or by violence to confiscate his estate, without accusation or trial, would be so gross and notorious an act of despotism, as must at once convey the alarm of tyranny throughout the whole kingdom. But confinement of the person, by secretly hurrying him to gaol, where his sufferings are unknown or forgotten; is a less public, a less striking, and therefore more dangerous engine of arbitrary government.... (Supreme Court 2004a, p. 555).

Unfortunately history has confirmed the many ways in which state violations of the human right to liberty have enabled officials to destroy democracy and inflict immense harms upon innocent individuals. Even weighed together, these values do not imply that the human right to liberty is absolute, that it is morally wrong to infringe it in every case. But it does show that there is a heavy burden of justification upon a state when it detains any human being.

Moreover, in most nation states the government is required to present at least a prima facie justification of its action soon after it detains anyone. Thus, Jose Padilla and Shafiq Rasul et. al. petitioned in United States district courts for a writ of habeas corpus. (Supreme Court 2004b). Habeas corpus is a writ in the common law tradition, subsequently recognized in acts of Parliament and in many national constitutions.

In national legal systems it serves to recognize and ensure the enjoyment of the human right recognized in Article 9.4 of the *International Covenant on Civil and Political Rights* (United Nations 1966b) that reads:

> Anyone who is deprived of his liberty by arrest or detention shall be entitled to take proceedings before a court, in order that that court may decide without delay on the lawfulness of his detention and order his release if the detention is not lawful.

And this international human right reflects in turn one element of the prior moral human right to due process.

After commenting on the three absolute common law rights of persons, presumed also to be fundamental moral rights, Blackstone observes:

> But in vain would these rights be declared, ascertained, and protected by the dead letter of the laws, if the constitution had provided no other method to secure their actual enjoyment. It has therefore established certain other auxiliary subordinate rights of the subject, which serve principally as outworks or barriers to protect and maintain inviolate the three great and primary rights, of personal security, personal liberty, and private property (Blackstone 1902, pp. 140–141).

Blackstone's explanation of the legal function of auxiliary rights such as the writ of habeas corpus points to the grounds of the moral right of any person detained by state action to a hearing to determine whether her detention is justified. These are the moral reasons that ground the fundamental moral right to liberty, for any reason sufficient to ground the moral human right to liberty must in turn be sufficient to justify a right that protects its enjoyment.

However, the moral right to due process is no more absolute than the fundamental moral right to liberty that it protects. How much due process, if any, is a state morally required to provide for a human being soon after she has been detained? Is a detainee entitled, as the *International Covenant on Civil and Political Rights* (United Nations 1966b) affirms, to take proceedings before a court that may decide without delay on the lawfulness of his detention? In her opinion in *Hamdi v. Rumsfeld*, Justice O'Connor explains how this question should be answered under United States law:

> *Mathews* dictates that the process due in any given instance is determined by weighing "the private interest that will be affected by the official action" against the Government's asserted interest, "including the function involved" and the burdens the Government would face in providing greater process (Supreme Court 2004a, p. 529).

Much the same procedure of weighing is the proper method to decide how much due process is morally due any detainee. In this case, what must be weighed is the seriousness of the infringement of Hamdi's right to liberty against the state's need to deny habeas corpus in order to prevent continuing terrorism. After balancing these two considerations, O'Connor, writing for the Supreme Court, concludes:

> We therefore hold that a citizen-detainee seeking to challenge his classification as an enemy combatant must receive notice of the factual basis for his classification, and a fair opportunity to rebut the Government's factual assertions before a neutral decision maker (Supreme Court 2004a, p. 533).

Then in the next paragraph she explains:

> At the same time, the exigencies of the circumstances may demand that, aside from these core elements, enemy-combatant proceedings may be tailored to alleviate their uncommon potential to burden the Executive at a time of ongoing military conflict.

For example, hearsay evidence that would normally be excluded might be introduced, and there might be a presumption in favor of the government's evidence. She thinks it unlikely that "this basic process" will have any dire impact upon the functions of making war against terrorists (Supreme Court 2004a, pp. 533–534). Obviously, weighing the complex conflicting considerations in any given case will be difficult and often controversial. Thus, Justice Thomas explains why he believes that the interest in national security outweighs Hamdi's right to due process under the circumstances of this case (Supreme Court 2004a, pp. 595–596).

For present purposes it is not necessary to decide whether Justice O'Connor or Justice Thomas weighed the legally relevant considerations more accurately. What we need to recognize is that there are at least two moral limits on the state's action of detaining individuals as a means of combating terrorism. These are the fundamental moral rights to liberty and to due process. Under some circumstances, however, detaining an individual and providing her with very little due process may be morally justified when this is necessary for some urgent state purpose.

Is there any moral limit on the length of time that a state may detain individuals as a means of combating terrorism? One morally problematic response to contemporary terrorism is indefinite detention. But in what sense of "indefinite" do states claim a right to subject human beings to indefinite detention? In every sense, indefinite detention is detention with no set time for release. But a significant ambiguity remains. Detention may be indefinite if the authorities are required to release the detainee when some specified condition not defined in temporal terms has been met, for example whenever one is no longer a danger to society. On the other hand, detention may be indefinite when the authorities have unlimited discretion as to both the time and the conditions for one's release.

The United States has claimed the right to hold individuals indefinitely in the more problematic sense of unconditional detention:

> The Government contends that Hamdi is an "enemy combatant," and that this status justifies holding him in the United States indefinitely—without formal charges or proceedings—unless and until it makes the determination that access to counsel or further process is warranted (Supreme Court 2004a, pp. 510–511).

In other words, it is up to the administration alone to decide when, if ever, to release Hamdi with no statutory limitations or oversight by the courts or other authorities. This is clearly a complete denial of due process to the detainee.

Presumably the state ought never to deprive any individual of her fundamental moral human rights without due process of law. This would be to subject the right-holder to arbitrary coercion and disregard the importance of human rights to the individual possessor. It is also morally dubious because of the importance of due process to society as a whole. As Justice Harlan explains:

> At its core, the right of due process reflects a fundamental value in our American constitutional system....Perhaps no characteristic of an organized and cohesive society is more fundamental than its erection and enforcement of a system of rules defining the various rights and duties of its members, enabling them to govern their affairs and definitely settle their differences in an orderly and predictable manner. Without such a "legal system," social organization and cohesion are virtually impossible; with the ability to seek regularized resolution of conflicts individuals are capable of interdependent action that enables them to strive for achievements without the anxieties that would beset them in a disorganized society (Supreme Court 1971, 374).

The tremendous value of the right to due process to individual persons and to society does not imply that it is morally impermissible to infringe it whatever the circumstances. But only extreme necessity could morally justify its complete denial, and surely a state is morally required to accord some limited measure of due process to almost any detainee.

On the other hand, it may be morally permissible for a state to detain individuals for an indefinite period of time provided it will release them when the appropriate conditions have been satisfied. What those conditions should be is determined by the purpose for which it is necessary to detain them. The obvious reason to detain an enemy combatant is to prevent him from engaging in or lending assistance to further terrorist attacks on the state or its citizens. If so, then presumably the state is morally required, as the Geneva Convention III asserts, to release the detainee "without delay after the cessation of hostilities." (United Nations 1949, Article 118) Unfortunately, some states are currently combating threats of serious terrorism with no end in sight. If so, they ought to apply the more basic moral condition that requires release of each detained individual when he is no longer likely to engage in or contribute to terrorism against the state. This is a moral as well as a legal requirement because when the legitimate reason to detain someone ends, then the justification for detention ends with it.

Another purpose for indefinite detention is to hold someone in order to extract information that is urgently needed to prevent or reduce the damage done by future terrorism. Since what justifies detention for this purpose is the necessity of knowing the identity, plans and abilities of enemy terrorists in order to counter the threat they pose, the state ought to release a detainee when interrogating him will no longer be fruitful. This will depend upon how much useful information the detainee has and how cooperative or uncooperative he may be. However, this will almost always be long before the serious threat of terrorism has been eliminated.

A third purpose for indefinite detention is to hold someone suspected of having engaged in criminal acts of terrorism until his trial. Presumably he ought to be released promptly if he is subsequently found not guilty or to be handed over to the appropriate authorities for punishment if convicted. But how long could a state justify detention for this purpose? Article 9.3 of the *International Covenant on Civil and Political Rights* (United Nations 1966b) reads in part:

> Anyone arrested or detained on a criminal charge should be brought promptly before a judge or other officer authorized by law to exercise judicial power and shall be entitled to trial within a reasonable time or to release.

A reasonable time in this regard is probably the length of time required for the state and the defendant to prepare their cases. Any unnecessary delay by either party would be unjustified. However, the state might delay the start of this process simply by not charging the detainee with any criminal offense. Presumably the state would be justified in doing so only until the detainee's moral right to habeas corpus or some comparable hearing becomes applicable, normally a relatively short time after being detained.

A related purpose for indefinite detention is to hold someone as a material witness in a trial of someone suspected of having engaged in criminal acts of terrorism. Since what justifies detention for this purpose is the need to convict and punish terrorists, both in ways that will prevent them from engaging in further terrorism and to deter others who might be motivated to do so, any material witness ought to be released as soon as she has testified or at least at the conclusion of the trial for which her testimony is needed.

Finally, an alien ordered to be deported as one suspected of being a terrorist or of aiding or abetting terrorism might be detained indefinitely if deportment proceedings could not be completed during the normal period of time. This sometimes happens because the state of which he or she is a citizen refused to grant reentry. Of course, someone might be detained for more than one legitimate state purpose. In that event, he ought to be released whenever all of these purposes have been served.

No doubt it will be difficult in many cases to know with any confidence whether indefinite detention is justified and when release is morally required. But two general principles are clear enough. There is a crucial moral distinction between indefinite detention in the sense that gives the state unlimited discretion as to when to release the detainee and indefinite detention in the sense that requires release when some specific condition has been satisfied. And the condition that morally requires release depends upon the purpose that justifies detention in the first place.

5.3 Interrogation

Everyone agrees that the interrogation of detained persons is necessary to gain information needed to combat the ongoing threat of terrorism. They also agree that some degree of pressure, even coercion, is necessary for the effective interrogation of terrorists or those sympathetic them. Both the United Kingdom, in Northern Ireland, and the United States, more recently, have used coercive interrogation.

> It quickly became clear that domestic intelligence agencies did not have sufficient information. The military took it upon itself to obtain it. To get detainees to talk, the security forces used five "deep interrogation" techniques: wall-standing, hooding, noise, a bread and water diet, and sleep deprivation.... (Donohue 2008, pp. 49–50). Then in April 2004 pictures of the abuses in Abu Ghraib burst upon the public. The Pentagon's immediate

defense of its practices (e.g., hooding, sleep and dietary deprivation, stress positions, isolation for more than 30 days, and intimidation using dogs), as being consistent with international law was met with skepticism, anger and outright condemnation (Donohue 2008, p. 100).

After 9/11, the scope and frequency of so-called extraordinary rendition (that is, the transfer of individuals not to stand criminal trial, but to be interrogated by other states "in circumstances that make it more likely than not that the individual will be subjected to torture or cruel, inhuman, or degrading treatment") expanded (Donohue 2008, p. 105).

However, there is serious disagreement about the moral limits on justifiable interrogation, especially whether the use of torture is ever morally justified.

A memorandum prepared by the Office of Legal Counsel for Alberto R. Gonzales, Counsel to the President, argues that it is sometimes legally justified.

We believe that a defense of necessity could be raised under the circumstances to an allegation of a Section 2340A violation [of its ban on torture]. Often referred to as the "choice of evils" defense, necessity has been defined as follows:Conduct that the actor believes to be necessary to avoid harm or evil to himself or to another is justifiable, provided that:

(a) the harm or evil sought to be avoided is greater than that sought to be prevented by the law defining the offense charged; and
(b) neither the Code nor other law defining the offense provides exceptions or defenses dealing with the specific situation involved; and
(c) a legislative purpose to exclude the justification claimed does not otherwise plainly appear (Greenberg and Dratel 2005, pp. 207–208).

This reasoning is analogous to the weighing of the moral urgency of the state action at issue against the seriousness of the infringement of the human right involved that often justifies surveillance that infringes the right to privacy or detention that infringes the right to liberty. Leaving aside the question of the soundness of this legal analysis, could interrogation by means of torture be morally justified in spite of the moral human right not to be tortured?

There are those who might deny this because they believe that, unlike the human rights to privacy and to liberty that may be infringed when exceptional circumstances make this necessary, the moral human right not to be tortured is absolute. Thus Joel Feinberg writes:

We should not despair, however, of finding explicit standards of (say) cruelty that will give human rights content and yet leave them plausible candidates for absoluteness in the strong sense. The right not to be tortured, for example, comes close to exhaustive definability in nonstandard-bearing terms, and may be such that it cannot conflict with other rights, including other human rights, and can therefore be treated as categorical and exceptionless (Feinberg 1973, p. 87).

If the moral human right not to be tortured is absolute in the strong sense implying that its infringement is morally wrong no matter what the circumstances, then the necessity to avoid harm, even catastrophic disaster, could never justify its violation. But is the moral human right not to be tortured really absolute?

The ticking bomb scenario shows that this is not so. David Luban explains the argument as follows:

> Suppose the bomb is planted somewhere in the crowded heart of an American city, and you have custody of the man who planted it. He won't talk. Surely, the hypothetical suggests, we shouldn't be too squeamish to torture the information out of him and save hundreds of lives. Consequences count, and abstract moral prohibitions must yield to the calculus of consequences (Luban 2005, p. 1440).

Hence, one would be morally justified in infringing the human right not to be tortured of a detained individual if this really were necessary to prevent a vastly greater moral evil.

Although there are those who believe that this hypothetical example is unrealistic, Luban reports that "in 1995, an al Queda plot to bomb eleven U.S. airliners and to assassinate the pope was thwarted by information tortured out of a Pakistani bomb-maker by the Philippine police" (Luban 2005, p. 1441). Presumably, their successful use of torture to combat terrorism was justified by its necessity given the circumstances.

What, then, should one say of the international human right not to be tortured? Article 1 of the *Convention against Torture and Other Cruel, Inhuman or Degrading Treatment or Punishment* (United Nations 1984) reads in part:

> For the Purposes of this Convention, the term "torture" means any act by which severe pain or suffering, whether physical or mental, is intentionally inflicted on a person for such purposes as obtaining from him...information...when such pain or suffering is inflicted by or at the instigation of or with the consent or acquiescence of a public official or other person acting in an official capacity.

Then Article 2.2 asserts categorically that "No exceptional circumstances whatsoever, whether a state of war or a threat of war, internal political instability or any other public emergency, may be invoked as a justification of torture." Hence, the international right not to be tortured is absolute because necessity can never render it permissible under international law. Ought international law to prohibit the use of torture in interrogation without exception when some such acts are morally justified? In a word, yes. Although the moral human right not to be tortured is not absolute, the international human right not to be tortured, and presumably the analogous right in national legal systems, ought morally to be absolute. This is because these legal rights, unlike the moral right not to be tortured, hold only against the state and its public officials.

But if it is morally permissible for public officials to balance the infringement of the human rights to privacy and liberty against the necessity of surveillance and detention to combat terrorism, why is it not morally permissible similarly for the state to use torture in interrogation when its necessity outweighs the seriousness of the infringement of the detainee's human right not to be tortured?

For one thing, the inherent harm of surveillance by intercepting one's e-mail, tapping one's phone or even installing hidden microphones and cameras in one's home is must less than the harm inherent in the use of torture in interrogation. To be sure, a person subject to surveillance may be seriously harmed if information gained is used to convict him of a crime or even released to the public so as to ruin his reputation. But these are indirect harms that those who conduct surveillance usually have no strong motive to inflict and that can in most cases be controlled by making such evidence inadmissible in a court of law and regulating the storage and transmission of information received. However, the use of torture is in and of itself seriously harmful, and it often inflicts secondary harms such as bodily injury and psychological trauma that are unavoidably tied to torture.

Even more important is the fact that unnecessary means of surveillance tend to be self-correcting while the use of torture in interrogation almost inevitably escalates even when unnecessary. Thus, if the surveillance of some individual over a period of time reveals no useful information, then public officials are much more likely to discontinue it than to intensify their efforts. But it is precisely when mildly coercive methods of interrogation fail to obtain the needed information that state officials begin to torture a detainee; and then when just a little torture proves ineffective, to turn to increasingly agonizing forms of torture with increasing danger of concomitant bodily and mental harm. Even the most conscientious interrogators have no reliable criteria to determine when the detainee is refusing to give them the information they need and when he has no useful information to give to them. Therefore, far from being self-correcting, the use of torture in tends to escalate in increasingly harmful ways (Luban 2005, p. 1447).

The inherent harm of detention is typically much greater than that imposed by surveillance because by its very nature it prevents the detainee from the interactions with family, friends and colleagues that enrich his life and from pursuing any of the ongoing projects that give meaning to his existence. Nor is it self-correcting in the way that surveillance usually is. However, it does not tend to escalate in the way that the use of torture in interrogation does, and its unnecessary use can be considerably restricted by due process of law. Thus, the infringement of the human right to liberty by detention is almost always a more serious wrong than the infringement of the human right to privacy by surveillance but less serious than the violation of the human right not to be tortured in interrogation. Therefore, it is morally permissible for state officials to weight the seriousness of infringing the right to liberty against necessity but not to torture on the pretext that this is justified by some compelling state need.

Moreover, official acceptance of torture in cases of extreme emergency breeds a culture of torture that spreads to borderline cases and far beyond. As David Luban explains:

> The liberal fiction that interrogation can be done by people who are neither cruel nor tyrannical runs aground on the fact that regardless of the interrogator's character off the job, on the job, every fiber of his concentration is devoted to dominating the mind of the subject. Only one thing prevents this from turning into abuse and torture, and that is a clear set of bright-line rules, drummed into the interrogator with the intensity of a religious indoctrination, complete with warnings of fire and brimstone. (Luban 2005, 1448) and
>
> My conclusion is very simple. Abu Ghraib is the fully predictable image of what a torture culture looks like. Abu Ghraib is not a few bad apples—it is the apple tree. And you cannot reasonable expect that interrogators in a torture culture will be the fastidious and well-meaning torturers that the liberal ideology fantasizes (Luban 2005, p. 1452).

Jeremy Waldron identifies a crucial cause of a torture culture:

> The important point is that the use of torture is not an area in which human motives are trustworthy. Sadism, sexual sadism, the pleasure of indulging brutality, the love of power, and the enjoyment of the humiliation of others—these all-too-human characteristics need to be kept tightly under control, especially in the context of war and terror, where many of the usual restraints on human action are already loosened (Waldron 2010, p. 221).

In short, the international human right not to be tortured and the analogous right in a national legal system ought to be absolute because to permit any exceptions would lead to a culture of torture that would motivate interrogators to inflict morally intolerable abuse upon many detainees.

Finally, the state is morally permitted to enforce its legal rules and regulations only because its legal system is not imposed upon its subjects, unlike the domination of the mafia over those it exploits, by brute force. Thus, for a state to recognize exceptions to the general legal prohibition against torture would be to undermine the spirit or character of morally justified law. Jeremy Waldron suggests this when he writes:

> The rule against torture is archetypical of a certain policy having to do with the relation between law and force, and with regard to the persons it rules. The prohibition on torture is expressive of an important underlying policy of the law, which we might try to capture in the following way: Law is not brutal in its operation; law is not savage; law does not rule through abject fear and terror, or by breaking the will of those whom it confronts. If law is forceful or coercive, it gets its way by methods which respect rather than mutilate the dignity and agency of those who are its subjects. (Waldron 2010, p. 232) And

> The damage done to our system of law by undermining the prohibition on torture is, I think, just like this. If we were to permit the torture of Al Qaeda and Taliban detainees, or if we were to define what most of us regard as torture as not really "torture" at all to enable our officials to inflict pain on them while questioning them,...maybe only a few score detainees would be affected in the first instance. But the character of our legal system would be corrupted. We would be moving from a situation in which our law had a certain character—a general virtue of non-brutality—to a situation in which that character would be compromised or corrupted by the permitting of this most brutal practice (Waldron 2010, p. 246).

For a number of reasons, therefore, the right not to be tortured ought morally to be absolute in national and international law. Although no one of these reasons alone is sufficient to establish this conclusion, together they demonstrate a pattern of rights violations and serious harms to individuals and social institutions that rules out any exceptions.

Is this also true of the human right not to be subjected to cruel, inhuman or degrading treatment or punishment? Although Article 2.2 of the *Convention against Torture and Other Cruel, Inhuman or Degrading Treatment or Punishment* (United Nations 1984) specifies that "no exceptional circumstances whatsoever...may be invoked as a justification of torture," Article 16 concerning cruel, inhuman or degrading treatment or punishment contains no such provision. How, then, do these two kinds of mistreatment differ? In a relevant case, the European Court of Human Rights expresses the view that "this distinction derives principally from a difference in the intensity of the suffering inflicted" (European Court of Human Rights 1978, pp. 66–67).

This interpretation seems to be confirmed by Article 1.2 of the General Assembly Resolution 3452 of 1975 that reads: "Torture constitutes an aggravated and deliberate form of cruel, inhuman or degrading treatment or punishment" (General Assembly 1975, p. 624). On this view, the reasons why the right not to be tortured ought to be absolute in international law and national legal systems have less weight when applied to the right not to be subjected to cruel, inhuman or degrading treatment.

Although subjecting a person to cruel, inhuman or degrading treatment harms that individual seriously, the inherent harm of such treatment is significantly less than that inflicted by torture. And the probability of collateral damage, either physiological injury or psychological trauma is markedly less. Hence, it is more likely that the urgency of state necessity could outweigh the seriousness of the infringement of this right than that of the violation of the right not to be tortured.

When interrogators use cruel, inhuman or degrading treatment to extract information from detainees, there is the same tendency of escalation as when they resort to torture. But if, and this is a big if, torture is prohibited even in the most extreme emergencies, then this danger will be limited. And if public policy and the training of interrogators and all those who have authority over detainees emphasize the absoluteness of the human right not to be tortured, there is much less chance that a culture of torture will develop.

But the most important difference is probably that the use of cruel, inhuman or degrading treatment as a method of interrogation does not undermine the nature of a morally permissible legal system in the way that the use of torture does. Any effective legal system will need to enforce its rules and regulations. Although this involves coercive measures that are prima facie wrong, these are morally permissible because they are necessary in order for the state to prevent serious harm to and protect the moral rights of its subjects. Similarly, the use of cruel, inhuman or degrading means of interrogation is very coercive. This is because they force the detainee to choose between the typically unwelcome and sometimes highly repugnant option of giving sensitive information to the interrogator and the option of undergoing the far worse suffering inflicted by cruel, inhuman or degrading treatment. One active in or sympathetic to terrorism who gave into such pressure might try to assuage his conscience or counter the criticism of others by thinking or saying, "but I had no choice." However, this would be only a figure of speech. He did have a choice, although one in which he was coerced into acting against his will. But the purpose of using torture as a means of interrogation is to break the will of the detainee so that he literally has no choice, to inflict such extreme pain and suffering upon the detainee that no strength of will could enable him to resist the will of the interrogator (Luban 2005, p. 1431). The brutality of torture is such that it excludes any rational weighing between options and thereby treats a human being as a brute animal. It is because the use of cruel, inhuman or degrading treatment in interrogation coerces but stops short of breaking the will of those subject to it that it need not undermine the moral justification of a legal system that permits it. Once more it is the cumulative force of these four considerations that explains why the right not to be tortured ought to be absolute in international law and national legal systems but the right not to be subjected to cruel, inhuman or degrading treatment may permit exceptions when it is necessary for some extremely urgent state purpose.

5.4 Trials

Whether or not terrorism is as such a national or international crime, terrorists use violent tactics that kill or maim innocent people and destroy property and thus act in ways that are typically criminal offences in national legal systems and often in international law also. Presumably to aid and abet such actions is also a crime. Hence, it is surely permissible and probably even morally required for any nation state to respond to terrorism by arresting and prosecuting anyone who engages in these criminal actions. But at this point, the state often faces a dilemma. If it introduces classified information in order to convict the accused, it will compromise its intelligence activities; but if it does not introduce secret information, then it will often be unable to convict individuals it has good reason to believe are terrorists or supporters of terrorism. Accordingly, a state might, as the United Kingdom and the United States have done, try terrorist suspects in special tribunals with procedural rules quite different from those required in its domestic courts.

The United Kingdom established special Diplock courts in Northern Ireland in 1973 to overcome widespread jury intimidation.

> Despite the advantages of the Diplock courts over internment, a crucial weakness of the new system was that it eliminated the defendant's peers from the courtroom. Perhaps most dramatically, the new system clashed with Britain's long tradition of the jury trial, which had come to symbolize the nation's embrace of liberty rights (Donohue 2008, pp. 45–46).

And in the United States, President Bush authorized the use of military commissions rather than the federal courts to try certain categories of terrorist suspects (Bush 2001, Sec. 4(a)).

On the assumption that international human rights are morally justified, the *International Covenant on Civil and Political Rights* (United Nations 1966b) specifies the moral limits on the use of special procedural rules in criminal cases regarding terrorism.

Article 14.1 of the *International Covenant* defines the most basic relevant procedural right as follows:

> In the determination of any criminal charge against him, or of his rights and obligations in a suit at law, everyone shall be entitled to a fair and public hearing by a competent, independent and impartial tribunal established by law.

The other provisions of this article specify various subsidiary due process rights that together help to ensure that any trial is in practice fair.

Central to this human right is the entitlement to a "fair and public hearing." The presupposition is that observation by the public, interested individuals and especially the press, will help to ensure that the trial is in fact fair and that the state does not abuse its power to unjustly disadvantage the defendant However, in Section 1(f) of the military order by which he authorized the use of military commissions to try suspected terrorists, President Bush found that:

> Given the danger to the safety of the United States and the nature of international terrorism, and to the extent provided by and under this order, I find consistent with section 836

> of title 10, United States Code, that it is not practicable to apply in military commissions under this order the principles of law and the rules of evidence generally recognized in the trial of criminal cases in the United States district courts (Bush 2001).

Therefore, he authorized the Secretary of Defense to issue special rules and regulations to govern these military commissions.

Subsequently the Secretary of Defense specified that in any trial of a Non-United States Citizen in the War against Terrorism, the military commission shall:

> Hold open proceedings except where otherwise decided by the Appointing Authority or the Presiding Officer in accordance with the President's Military Order and this Order. Grounds for closure include the protection of information classified or classifiable under reference (d); information protected by law or rule from unauthorized disclosure; the physical safety of participants in Commission proceedings, including prospective witnesses; intelligence and law enforcement sources, methods or activities; and other national security interests (United States 2002, Section 6B).

Although this procedural rule is susceptible to abuse by a presiding officer who sees his overriding duty to be combating international terrorism, it may not be morally unjustified.

Article 14.1 of the *International Covenant on Civil and Political Rights* (United Nations 1966b) that asserts the fundamental procedural right to a fair and open hearing continues:

> The press and the public may be excluded from all or part of a trial for reasons of morals, public order (*ordre public*) or national security in a democratic society, or when the interest of the private lives of the parties so requires, or to the extent strictly necessary in the opinion of the court in special circumstances where publicity would prejudice the interests of justice;...

Therefore, closing a trial to the public need not violate the defendant's human right to a fair and public hearing when this really is necessary in the interest of national security. This will often be the case in trials of those suspected of engaging in or aiding and abetting terrorism.

Closing a trial to the public is one thing; excluding the accused is quite another. Section 6B of the Secretary of Defense's *Military Commission Order No. 1* (United States 2002) reads in part as follows:

> A decision to close a proceeding or portion thereof may include a decision to exclude the Accused, Civilian Defense Counsel, or any other person, but the Detailed Defense Counsel may not be excluded from any trial proceeding or portion thereof. Except with the prior authorization of the Presiding Officer and subject to Section 9, Defense Counsel may not disclose any information presented during a closed session to individuals excluded from such proceeding or part thereof.

It is probably true that it will sometimes be necessary to exclude the accused and his civilian defense counsel, who may not have security clearance, in the interests of national security. But permitting only the Detailed Defense Counsel, who must be a United States military officer, to be present to represent the accused is surely not sufficient to ensure that the tribunal remains impartial and that the defendant receives a fair trial.

This procedural rule clearly infringes upon a crucial subsidiary due process right of the accused, the human right "to be tried in his presence, and to defend himself in person or through legal assistance of his own choosing…." (United Nations 1966a, Article 14.3(e)) Note that this is not the right to be present or to defend himself through legal assistance; it is the human right both to be present and to defend himself in person or through legal assistance of his own choosing. It is morally problematic that his Civilian Defense Counsel, whom he has chosen, may be excluded and only his Detailed Defense Counsel, who is chosen by the Chief Defense Counsel who will be a judge advocate of one of the United States armed forces, may be present at a hearing from which the accused is excluded. It is also morally problematic that his Detailed Defense Counsel may be, and usually will be, prohibited from informing him of any information presented during a closed hearing from which he has been excluded. This will at best severely compromise his subsidiary human right "to examine, or have examined, the witnesses against him." Because his guilt or innocence will depend upon establishing facts about his past actions, he is in a privileged position to know how to cross examine, or advise his counsel on how to cross examine, witnesses against him or to rebut other evidence introduced by the Prosecutor. Since the essential purpose of due process rights such as these is to ensure that the tribunal remains impartial and the trial fair, only very urgent necessity could justify the use of any procedural rule that excludes the defendant from a hearing closed to the public or that prohibits informing him of any and all information presented during a hearing from which he has been excluded (Supreme Court 2006, pp. 623–625).

Still, there could be and probably are occasions when the disclosure of classified information concerning terrorism would threaten national security to such an extent that it would be morally justifiable to exclude the accused from a hearing and prohibit his defense counsel from disclosing to him classified information presented during his absence. However, there is a considerable danger that the authority to exclude the accused from a hearing will be abused by an over zealous presiding officer or, even if properly used, that it will prejudice the trial against the defendant. Therefore, another human due process right is crucially important. Article 14.5 of the *International Covenant on Civil and Political Rights* (United Nations 1966b) reads: "Everyone convicted of a crime shall have the right to his conviction and sentence being reviewed by a higher tribunal according to law."

Justice Stevens succinctly describes the review procedures granted to the accused by the Secretary of Defense's *Military Commission Order No. 1* as follows:

> Any appeal is taken to a three-member review panel composed of military officers and designated by the Secretary of Defense, only one of which need have experience as a judge. §6(H)(4). The review panel is directed to "disregard any variance from procedures specified in this Order or elsewhere that would not materially have affected the outcome of the trial before the Commission." *Ibid.* Once the panel makes its recommendation to the Secretary of Defense, the Secretary can either remand for further proceedings or forward the record to the President with his recommendation as to final disposition. §6(H)(5). The President then, unless he has designated the task to the Secretary, makes the "final decision." §6(H)(6) (Supreme Court 2006, p. 615).

This very limited right of appeal is obviously inadequate to protect the human right of the accused to a review of his conviction and sentence. The impartiality of a review panel composed of United States military officers designated by the Secretary of Defense, even if they all have had experience as a judge, is open to serious doubt. And that the final decision should be made by the President, acting in his capacity as Commander in Chief of the armed forces combating terrorism, or his Secretary of Defense, whose primary obligation is to defend the United States against any and all armed attacks including those by terrorists, can by no stretch of the imagination be construed to be a decision by an impartial tribunal. It seems undeniable that any morally justified review process should include a right to appeal to some regularly constituted court, presumably in the first instance a United States district court.

But would this not unjustifiably imperil national security by disclosing highly sensitive intelligence to persons without security clearance? Probably not, or at worst only very rarely. For one thing, and not merely incidentally, the prospect of a rigorous review would motivate the presiding officer of any military commission to exclude the accused only when absolutely necessary, thus reducing the number of appeals to a civilian court. Moreover, there will almost always be a considerable time lag between the detention of a suspect and any subsequent appeal. The state will typically delay for a reasonable, often an unreasonable, time before charging him with criminal action, and the preparations for and proceedings during his trial will take considerable additional time. Hence, most classified information presented at the trial will have lost its importance for preventing potential terrorism. Finally, because there is no jury present during the proceedings before a court of appeals and in cases where state secrets are relevant the court can and presumably would be closed to the public, classified information need be disclosed only to the judge or judges hearing the case. Even if they do not have the highest security clearance, they tend to be conscientious and conservative persons who are most unlikely to betray state secrets. These considerations weaken the moral force of necessity so much that it can no longer outweigh the moral force of the human right to a review before an impartial tribunal. Therefore, although it is morally permissible to try anyone suspected of criminal action associated with terrorism in a special tribunal such as a military commission and to use special rules of procedure in the conduct of the trial, in the end anyone convicted and sentenced by such a tribunal ought morally to have a legal right of appeal to a regularly constituted court that will accord him more adequate due process rights.

5.5 Targeted Killing

Both Israel and the United States have responded to the threat of terrorism by targeting and killing leading terrorists. As Michael L. Gross reports:

> Faced with increasing terror attacks on civilians and a growing network of armed Palestinian militias, assassination or 'targeted killings' offered military planners what appeared to be an effective way to limit collateral damage while crippling militia

> leadership and eliminating those responsible for terror attacks. These goals were consistent with Israel's larger military aims of maintaining national security, minimizing casualties, preventing the erosion of ground positions and bringing the Palestinians back to the negotiating table (Gross 2003, p. 351).

Although the United States originally condemned this policy, it seems to have more recently adopted a very similar one. In 2011, United States navy seals killed Osama bin Laden in a commando raid in Pakistan, United States drones killed Anwar Awlaki and subsequently Ibrahim al-Banna together with six other suspected terrorists in Yemen. As one would expect, these policies have elicited considerable criticism. Because those more knowledgeable about international and national law disagree about its legality, I will limit myself to a consideration of the most relevant moral considerations.

The usual justification for any targeting killing of a leading terrorist is that this is an exercise of the state's moral right to self-defense. Strictly speaking, this is the right of a sovereign state to use all necessary force to respond to an attack that threatens its very existence. Although Israel could plausibly use this justification against the threat of Hamas, the United States would have to fall back upon its moral right to protect its citizens from severe harms and the violation of their human rights, and Israel could buttress its justification by appealing to this right also. These moral rights are surely relevant to the threat of terrorism and might justify at least some targeted killings.

However, these moral rights to self-defense are not unlimited. For one thing, a state may use lethal force to defend itself or its citizens only when this is necessary, when there is no less harmful alternative. If, for example, it were possible to capture and detain a dangerous terrorist, then assassination would be unjustified. However, this is very seldom practicable. As Daniel Statman observes:

> The standard means of fighting crime also seem unaccommodating in the face of this threat; the chances of Interpol capturing Bin Laden and his followers and bringing them to justice are remote, as are the chances of the Israeli police arresting and trying the leaders of Hammas and Islamic Jihad (Statman 2004, p. 179).

Hence, this alternative to the use of force in self-defense is typically not viable.

Another alternative might be to negotiate with the terrorist group threatening violent action against a nation state. No doubt politicians often exaggerate the futility of negotiation with terrorists, but more often terrorists who are capable of inflicting serious harm on a nation state are fanatical about their cause and unwilling even to consider a reasonable compromise. A State could, presumably, avoid future attacks by submitting to every demand of the terrorists. But for Israel to accept the demand of Hamas for the annihilation of the Jewish state would hardly be a measure of self-defense. And for the United States to abandon Israel and its other allies in the Middle East might well be to sacrifice some of its most vital interests and, in any event, pave the way for fundamentalist Islamic regimes like that of the Taliban that would violate the human rights of their citizens on a massive scale. Daniel Statman rightly argues that this is not a morally required option.

> In all these cases, the question is not whether the aggressor's demands could be accommodated without the use of force, but whether such accommodation would be morally acceptable—and the answer seems to be in the negative. Yielding to Hammas in order to prevent their murderous attacks is no more acceptable than yielding to Bin Laden (Statman 2004, p. 194).

I agree that in many cases negotiation is not a morally acceptable alternative to the use of force in response to terrorism.

A second limitation on the moral rights of a nation state to use force in response to the threat of serious harm to itself or its citizens is that some violent attack must be imminent. There are those who interpret this limitation to require that in the absence of defensive action the attack would take place in the immediate future. However, Tamar Meisels rejects this interpretation.

> Most targeted killings, admittedly, are not carried out in the face of immediate danger, nor do operational difficulties always entail immediate action. A direct appeal to "self-defense" as warrant for targeting wanted terrorists may still be justified even when the threat is less than outright and present, so long as the danger is nonetheless clear and imminent (Meisels 2008, pp. 145–146).

Although she does not explain her interpretation of the limitation to imminent threat, she does note that it applies to "the case of an active terrorist commander who continues to instigate dangerous terrorist attacks" (Meisels 2008, p. 146).

How should one interpret the requirement of imminence in order to capture its moral force? What is morally relevant is not the time of the attack a state is attempting to prevent, but whether it would in fact occur were the state not to prevent it by the use of force. And since waiting until the attack has taken place would render the right of self-defense futile, morality can require only that the state officials be reasonably certain of this fact. Hence, Meisels seems correct in suggesting that this fits the case of at least some terrorist leaders who are actively engaged in planning and expediting an ongoing series of violent attacks.

Whether this is sufficient to justify targeted killings remains controversial. One might well argue that although a nation state is morally justified in using force to prevent imminent terrorist attacks, this does not justify targeted killings because these violate fundamental human rights, Specifically:

> It violates the right of suspects to a fair trial and affects the presumption of innocence…; somebody who is accused of being a terrorist, even if he has participated in terrorist activities in the past, should have a right to a fair trial where his sentence would be decided in a court of law (Lekea 2003, p. 232).

And as Amnesty International has insisted, "It cancels the prohibition against the prohibition against the arbitrary deprivation of life that cannot be derogated from in any circumstances, even in a time of national emergency" (Lekea 2003, p. 232). In brief, targeted killings violate both the human right to due process and the human right to life. Presumably these are fundamental moral rights as well as rights in international law.

However, the human right to due process is relevant only to cases when an individual is accused of wrongdoing and subject to punishment. But targeted killings are justified, if at all, as preventive actions not as deserved punishments. And Tamar Meisels dismisses the presumption of innocence as irrelevant to the usual instances of targeted killings. "I assume here, further, that there is usually little doubt as to the culpability of the pursued targets. Normally, the perpetrators themselves accept responsibility (as opposed to guilt)—bin Laden or Hamas, to cite extreme examples" (Meisels 2008, p. 130). Still, any use of lethal force does seem to violate the right to life of the person killed. Nevertheless, it seems morally justified when it is strictly necessary to prevent an attack that would violate human rights to a much greater extent, something true of many serious acts of terrorism. Thus, the moral duty of any nation state to protect its citizens from serious harms and the violation off their human rights might well justify some targeted killings.

However, this would be true only if targeted killings do in fact protect the citizens of a nation state from at least some terrorist attacks. Hence, the efficacy of targeted killings is relevant to their moral justifiability. Gross argues that targeted killings are in fact counterproductive. He admits that with respect to collateral damage, they are preferable to large-scale military action against terrorist bases. But he insists that this is outweighed by other factors.

> On the other hand, it is easy to see that assassinations are often followed by waves of terrorist attacks on Israeli citizens. The connection is increasingly evident as the conflict continues….Assassination not only brings about large number of Israeli casualties, but it undermines local Palestinian leadership, leading militant organizations to replace their depleted ranks with ever more radical leaders (Gross 2003, p. 357).

Hence, targeted killings cannot be justified by any appeal to self-defense.

Daniel Statman replies that targeted killings can be and often are an effective means of self-defense.

> First, in the war against terror, just as in the war against the mafia, what counts are the long-term results, not the immediate ones. In the short run, acts of revenge might follow the killing of terrorists, but in the long run, there is good reason to believe that such killings will weaken the terror organizations, generate demoralization among their members, force them to restrict their movements, and so on. The personal charisma and professional skills of the leaders and key figures of certain organizations are crucial to the success of their organizations, something that especially true with regard to terror organizations that operate underground with no clear institutional structure. It is reasonable to assume that killing such individuals will gradually make it more difficult for the terror machinery to function (Statman 2004, p. 192).

Unfortunately, I lack the detailed empirical information and the scientific ability to interpret it so as to secede whether in fact targeted killings are every effective. However, it does seem reasonable to believe that they might be in some instances and that in such cases targeted killings might well be morally justified.

There is one more consideration that calls for examination. Targeted killings are typically extraterritorial actions, state responses outside the territory over which a nation state claims sovereignty. As such, they are normally intrusions into the territory of another sovereign state. This raises both legal and moral questions.

5.6 Intrusion

Although some terrorist threats are domestic, today the most serious danger to any nation or its nationals comes from international terrorism. The majority of terrorist attacks and those that are most destructive of persons and property are inspired by and initiated by individuals, informal groups or organizations abroad. Hence, it would seem that to combat terrorism effectively it is necessary for a state to take preventive action outside of its own territory. It will be useful to distinguish between intrusions and invasions. An intrusion is an uninvited action of one state within the territory of another state. United States drone attacks upon suspected terrorists in Pakistan and the killing of Osama bin Laden by United States navy SEALs as well as its targeted killings of leading terrorists in Yemen are clearly examples. Although Palestine is not a sovereign state, Israeli military strikes into its territory to eliminate the bases of its rocket attacks and the targeted killings of Hamas terrorists seem morally very similar. A much more extensive intrusion into a nation state has been the United States missile strikes and the NATO bombing in Libya in support of forces attempting to oust Muammar al-Qaddafi. An invasion is a military campaign of one or more states using ground forces to take control of some or all of the territory of another state, for example the United States invasion of Afghanistan in 2001 and Iraq in 2003.

State responses to terrorism of these kinds are morally problematic both because they take place outside the territory of the responding state and because they intrude into the territory of another state. Article I of the *Montevideo Convention on Rights and Duties of States* Organization of American States 1933) provides: "The State as a person of international law should possess the following qualifications: (a) a permanent population; (b) a defined territory; (c) government; and (d) capacity to enter into relations with other States." One reason, although not the only one, for including a defined territory in the criteria for statehood is that states claim sovereignty.

Sovereignty is a complex of rights, but these can be divided into two clusters constituting internal sovereignty and external sovereignty respectively. This distinction is implicit in the *Charter of the United Nations*:

> According to a widely shared view, sovereignty has two complementary and mutually dependent dimensions: within a State, a sovereign power makes law with the assertion that this law is supreme and ultimate, i.e. that its validity does not depend on any other, or 'higher', authority. Externally, a sovereign power obeys no other authority (Simma 2002, p. 70).

Thus, each nation state claims both political authority, the supreme right to make and enforce law within its territory, and political independence, the right that no other state interfere with the exercise of its political authority. These are certainly rights recognized in international law and probably moral rights as well.

What grounds internal sovereignty, the moral right of a state to make and enforce law within its territory? What justifies a government in imposing legal regulations that restrict the liberty of its subjects and enforcing the law with sanctions such as fines, imprisonment or even death that infringe their human rights to property, liberty and life? It is the fact that without law and order, in what was traditionally called the state of nature, the population living there would be immensely more vulnerable to being harmed and having their moral rights violated by antisocial individuals or gangs. Thus, the political authority of a state is morally justified by the way in which its legal system protects its population from harm, and especially from violation of their human rights. Conversely, a state that rules by brute force, thereby violating the rights of its subjects and arbitrarily harming them, lacks political authority.

But why should this right to govern a population be defined territorially? It is partly because, although threats to members of its society may originate abroad, the proximate cause of any harm suffered or rights violation is necessarily precisely that, a nearby cause. Hence, a government can reliably protect its population only if it has effective control within the area in which the members of the society live and interact. Moreover, protection at a distance becomes rapidly less effective as the distance increases. It is no accident that the modern nation state originated with the development of centralized political governments at the same time that the control of the Holy Roman Empire lessened and the authority of the Roman Catholic Church was often repudiated. Given this fragmentation, the justifications of political authority are grounded on limited areas of the earth's surface. Hence, it would seem that any extraterritorial action of a state in response to the threat of terrorism would be morally problematic because it could not be justified as an exercise of its political authority.

A secondary ground of the state's internal sovereignty is probably the right of its population to self-determination. Article 1.1 of both the *International Covenant on Economic, Social and Cultural Rights* (United Nations 1966a) and the *International Covenant on Civil and Political Rights* (United Nations 1966b) assert: "All peoples have the right of self-determination. By virtue of that right they freely determine their political status and freely pursue their economic, social and cultural development." This right presumably implies that when a people have organized themselves into a nation state, no other state may interfere with the exercise of its political authority, for any such interference would not be determined by the people itself. And external sovereignty in turn grounds a moral right of territorial integrity of each state.

Moreover, external sovereignty is morally grounded upon the fact that no state can govern effectively if its internal control can be limited or disrupted by external interference. Hence, any intrusion reduces the ability of a nation state to protect its subjects from harm and from the violation of their human rights. In other words, the external sovereignty of a state is directly grounded upon the fact that it is a necessary condition of the effective exercise of its moral right to political authority and, thus, indirectly upon the grounds of its internal sovereignty.

This does not imply that extraterritorial responses to terrorism are always morally wrong, but it does show that they require some robust justification. The most obvious moral justification, and the one that states most often assert, is the right of self-defense. But precisely what does this right entitle a state to defend? Although this clearly permits a state to take whatever measures are necessary to preserve its very existence, terrorism seldom endangers the continued existence of a state. More plausibly, a state can claim that terrorist violence threatens one or more of its vital interests. However, it is all too easy to allege that some moderately important state interest is truly vital, essential to its very life or wellbeing. Finally, international law and morality have long recognized the right of any nation state to protect its nationals even when traveling or residing abroad. These distinctions concerning what a state has a right to defend remind one that the state's right of self-defense constitutes a justification ranging from very strong to relatively weak and that the moral justification of any extraterritorial response to terrorism is limited by the principle of proportionality. Any defensive actions must not harm persons or property or violate human rights more than the imminent terrorist attacks would if they were not combated.

Against whom does a state have a right to defend itself? Presumably the terrorists who are threatening its existence, interests or nationals. But these are individual persons, typically members of more or less tightly organized groups, but not members of the armed forces of any nation state. How, then, can a state's right to self-defense permit extraterritorial action that will violate the external and internal rights to sovereignty of another state? Some terrorism is state sponsored or at least state tolerated. If so, a state might claim that intrusions into the territory of another state is justified because that state is morally implicated in the terrorist attacks against which it is defending itself. Even if the other state is not actively supporting or passively tolerating the terrorists, a state may claim a right to defend itself by extraterritorial responses because the terrorist threats are not effectively suppressed by the state from which they arise. Here, as elsewhere, it is the necessity of some action with a legitimate purpose that justifies it, at least as long as that action is strictly necessary and not merely advantageous.

The necessity of extraterritorial responses to terrorism may be temporary. Article 51 of the *Charter of the United Nations* (United Nations 1945) reads in part:

> Nothing in the present Charter shall impair the inherent right of individual or collective self-defense if an armed attack occurs against a Member of the United Nations, until the Security Council has taken measures necessary to maintain international peace and security.

Presumably the "inherent right" of self-defense is a moral right, not merely a right recognized in customary international law. But this right is limited to circumstances in which there are not effective legal institutions sufficient to protect states from threats to their national security. Unfortunately, the international community has not yet created any institutions capable of extinguishing or even greatly reducing the threat of international terrorism. Hence, extraterritorial responses to terrorism, especially intrusions, sometimes remain justified by a state's right of self-defense, although only within the limits of proportionality and strict necessity.

5.7 Invasion

Invasion is very different matter. When resisted, as it almost always is, it results in a large number of casualties, human beings killed or injured, and the destruction of much valuable property. And to the extent that the invading forces manage to take control of territory within the invaded country, that nation becomes completely unable to exercise its internal sovereignty within those areas. Therefore, the serious harms inflicted upon both the citizens of the invaded nation and the invading forces as well as the sovereignty of the invaded nation limit the justification of any invasion. Clearly, any invading nation carries a very heavy burden of justification.

Nevertheless, the United States and its allies have twice responded to terrorist attacks or the prospect of them by invading a sovereign state. After the 9/11 attacks on the twin towers and the pentagon, the United States demanded that the Taliban extradite Osama Bin Laden for trial in the United States. When the Taliban repeated refused to do so, the United States and its allies first began air strikes on October 7, 2001 and later sent in ground troops to take the key cities of Afghanistan. Similarly, on March 19, 2003, the United States and its allies launched an air strike on Saddam Hussein's presidential palace and the next day sent in ground forces to defeat the Iraqi armed forces and occupy the country.

How, if at all, could these invasions be morally justified? Let us begin by considering the invasion of Afghanistan. The obvious justification is self-defense.

President Bush made this explicit in one of the principles of his national security strategy.

> **Prevent attacks by terrorists before they occur**. A government has no higher obligation than to protect the lives and livelihoods of its citizens. The hard core of the terrorists cannot be deterred or reformed; they must be tracked down, killed, or captured. They must be cut off from the network of individuals and institutions on which they depend for support. That network must in turn be deterred, disrupted, and disabled by using a broad range of tools (Bush 2006, p. 12).

This would seem to justify an incursion, sending in a small force to capture or kill Osama Bin Laden, but why was an invasion necessary?

Perhaps this is because the Taliban governed Afghanistan and was resisting the attempt of the United States to bring Bin Laden to trial. Hence, Bush enunciated another strategic principle.

> **Deny terrorists the support and sanctuary of rogue states**. The United States and its allies in the War on Terror make no distinction between those who commit acts of terror and those who support and harbor them, because they are equally guilty of murder. Any government that chooses to be an ally of terror, such as Syria or Iran, has chosen to be an enemy of freedom, justice, and peace. The world must hold those regimes to account (Bush 2006, p. 12).

Precisely how invading Afghanistan would hold the Taliban to account is unclear, but at least one can understand that its support for terrorism made Afghanistan a rogue state and thus undermined its external sovereignty, its moral right against intervention by other nation states.

But the serious harms inflicted upon the people of Afghanistan by the invasion remain to be justified. President Bush seemed to believe that in the long run these would be greatly outweighed by the benefits of regime change, replacing a brutal tyranny with a democratic government. If his prediction proves accurate, then the invasion of Afghanistan may have been morally justified, but today this is far from evident.

The Bush administration alleged that Iraq had ties with al-Qaeda. If this were true, it might well have justified the invasion of Iraq in much the way that it might have justified the invasion of Afghanistan. The United States and its allies might have been acting in self-defense against potential attacks by a powerful terrorist network, holding a nation state that sponsors terrorists accountable, and replacing a brutal tyranny with a democratic government. Moreover, the justificatory strength of these considerations might have been magnified by the increased danger posed by the alleged weapons of mass destruction—chemical, biological and especially nuclear. Here another principle of the Bush strategy is relevant.

> **Deny WMD to rogue states and to terrorist allies who would use them without hesitation.** Terrorists have a perverse moral code that glorifies deliberately targeting innocent civilians. Terrorists try to inflict as many casualties as possible and seek WMD to this end. Denying terrorists WMD will require new tools and new international approaches. We are working with partner nations to improve security at vulnerable nuclear sites worldwide and bolster the ability of states to detect, disrupt, and respond to terrorist activity involving WMD (Bush 2006, p. 12).

If necessary, this might even require invading a nation state that is seeking to develop and may even now possess weapons of mass destruction. The adequacy of this justification depends, of course, on whether in fact Iraq did have ties with al-Qaeda and was actually developing weapons of mass destruction with the intension of using them against the United States and its allies.

After both of these allegations were discredited, some persisted in claiming that the invasion of Iraq was morally justified on humanitarian grounds. Saddam Hussein's repressive policies were notorious and his massive slaughter of Kurds was clear evidence that he would go to any lengths to retain power and pursue his policies. Hence, his gross violations of human rights would presumably continue until there was a regime change in Iraq. Since internal opposition lacked the power to oust him, invasion by external powers seemed to be necessary to protect the human rights of the people of Iraq. However, it is not clear that Hussein's human rights violations were massive enough to justify a humanitarian intervention on the scale of invading and occupying the country. In any event, one can see that invasions require justification because they may violate the moral right of external sovereignty of a nation state and certainly do inflict grievous harm upon many of the invading forces and even more of the people living in the invaded country. And an invading nation might justify its action by appealing to self-defense and the protection of human rights.

5.8 Just Cause

In the usual sense, "just cause" refers to one of the *jus ad bellum* conditions in traditional and contemporary just war theories. It is one of the necessary, but not sufficient conditions for going to war against another nation state. Because terrorists engage in violent actions, often killing or severely injuring many victims and state responses are often equally if not more violent, it seems relevant to both terrorism and counter-terrorism. In a broader, but still relevant sense, "just war" refers to the reasons that might justify acts of terrorism or state responses to them. Thus, just cause is ambivalent. A nation state can appeal to it to justify its responses, even military actions, against terrorists or those who support terrorism and terrorists or states that sponsor terrorism can claim that it justifies engaging in or supporting terrorist violence.

This chapter has been primarily concerned with both the moral limits on state responses to terrorism and with the just causes that might outweigh these limits. However, there are those who argue that an additional moral limit on the justified actions of any nation state against terrorism is a just cause for which terrorists or those who support terrorism are acting. Is this view morally sound?

Although the General Assembly of the United Nations has repeatedly condemned terrorism, it has attempted to distinguish it from the justified use of political violence. The preface to a resolution concerning measures to prevent international terrorism reads in part:

> Reaffirming also the inalienable right to self-determination and independence of all peoples under colonial and racist regimes and other forms of alien domination and foreign occupation, and upholding the legitimacy of their struggle, in particular the struggle of national liberation movements, in accordance with the purposes and principles of the Charter and Declaration on Principles of International Law concerning Friendly Relations and Co-operation among States in accordance with the Charter of the United Nations (General Assembly 1989, Preface).

Thus, plausible examples of terrorism with a just cause might be the struggle of Algerian freedom fighters against French colonialism, campaigns of terror by the African National Congress to end apartheid in South Africa, and terrorism of the Palestine Liberation Organization after June 1967 when Israel occupied much of the Egyptian Sinai, the Syrian Golan Heights and the Palestinian West Bank.

Granted that terrorists may sometimes be fighting against grave injustices, it does not follow that their violent tactics are morally justified. Sometimes they might be able to promote their just cause as effectively by nonviolent political action, and often the harms and rights violations imposed by their violent means may be disproportionate to their just end. Nor does the justice of their cause eliminate or even reduce the justifications of the state responses previously assessed. States are morally permitted and usually obligated to protect themselves and their nationals from grave harm and the violation of their rights. However, it does justify the General Assembly resolution that:

> *Urges* all States, unilaterally and in co-operation with other States, as well as relevant United Nations organs, to contribute to the progressive elimination of the causes underlying international terrorism and to pay special attention to all situations, including colonialism, racism and situations involving mass and flagrant violations of human rights and fundamental freedoms and those involving alien domination and foreign occupation, that may give rise to international terrorism and may endanger international peace and security (General Assembly 1989, Article 6).

Therefore, the fact that the terrorists attacking a state may have a just cause imposes no further moral limits on the preventive actions it is permitted to take against the terrorists, but it does make it morally impermissible for the state to combat the terrorists without also combating the injustices for which they are fighting.

If a state were to engage in strenuous good-faith efforts to eliminate the injustices that cause and may even justify terrorism, one would hope that the threat of terrorism would end and preventive measures would no longer be necessary. But terrorists are often fanatics who mistakenly believe that their cause is just. The militant wing of Hamas insists that the creation of Israel was contrary to international law and that its continued existence is a grave injustice against the Palestinian people and their Muslim religion. Let us suppose, for the sake of argument, that this is not true. If so, then the Hamas terrorists are not fighting for a just cause. But it may still be true that the continuing plight of the Palestinian refugees is a gross injustice that would be a just cause for their terrorism. How ought Israel, and its ally the United States, to respond? They would be morally justified in taking effective measures to protect themselves against the potential harms and rights violations of Hamas. And although they would not be morally required to seek to dismantle the state of Israel, they ought morally to make every effort to alleviate the suffering of the Palestinian refugees and to create a viable Palestinian state that could be their homeland. In other words, what is relevant to the morally justified state responses to terrorism is not whether the terrorists that threaten the state believe that their cause is just, but that in fact there is a cause that would justify their terrorism.

5.9 General Conclusions

A nation state has political authority, the moral right to make and enforce rules and regulations governing all individuals within its territory, primarily because of the way in which it protects its subjects from serious harms and especially from violations of their human rights. Hence, it is morally required to take effective measures to prevent attacks by international or domestic terrorists. But there are moral limits to permissible state responses to the threat of terrorism. Foremost among these are the human rights upon which its political authority is grounded.

Surveillance, detention and harsh interrogation often infringe the human rights to privacy, liberty and freedom from torture respectively. In fact, each of these may indirectly infringe other human rights as well, for example the rights to freedom of expression, freedom of association and to political participation. Accordingly, any state response to terrorism must respect the principle of proportionality. The seriousness of its infringement of human rights must be weighed against and must not exceed the urgency of the justifying state purpose or purposes. Moreover, any infringement of human rights must be strictly necessary for the promotion or preservation of these legitimate state purposes. A state response is morally impermissible if there is some alternative measure that would be equally effective with less or no infringement of the human rights of those affected.

Any kind of state response to terrorism may serve more than one state purpose. For example, the detention of individuals may be necessary to obtain information from them needed to anticipate and counteract future terrorism, to restrain individuals so that they cannot engage in or support terrorism, or to imprison those guilty of past acts of terrorism for trial, or to hold material witnesses whose testimony is needed in the trial of one or more suspected terrorists. Although each of these is a legitimate state purpose, they may impose different limits on justified detention. Detention to prevent a detainee from engaging in terrorism lasts only as long as the threat of continued terrorism exists. Someone held as a material witness ought to be released as soon as the trial in which she is to be a witness has been held. And anyone held for interrogation may be detained only as long as there is any reasonable prospect of obtaining additional useful information from him.

Although the primary grounds of any moral human right are the harms the individual right-holder would suffer were it denied or limited, it may also be grounded upon its importance to society in general. Thus, both the right not to be subjected to torture and the right to due process when one is before a court or tribunal contribute to the ideal rule of law that enhances the quality of life for all those in the society subject to a legal system.

Finally, morally relevant considerations will limit justified state responses in different ways. The right to privacy might limit the means used in surveillance or the kinds of information that may be collected or the ways in which collected information may be subsequently used. And although human rights typically limit state responses negatively by ruling out some kinds of state actions, any just cause for which terrorists may be fighting adds a positive moral requirement, that the state take steps to eliminate or reduce the injustices against which the terrorists are struggling.

References

Blackstone Sir William (1902) Commentaries on the Laws of England, ed William Draper. Philadelphia, Rees Welsh

Bush GW (2001) Detention, treatment and trial of certain non-citizens in the war against terrorism. 66 Fed Reg 37833

Bush GW (2006) The National Security Strategy of the United States. Available on the web at national security strategy 2006 pdf

Council of Europe (1950) European convention for the protection of human rights and fundamental freedoms. CETS No.: 005

Donohue LK (2008) The cost of counterterrorism: power, politics, and liberty. Cambridge University Press, Cambridge

European Court of Human Rights (1978) Case of England v. the United Kingdom. A. 25(1978) 2 EHRH 25

Feinberg J (1973) Social philosophy. Prentice-Hall, Engelwood Cliffs

General Assembly (1948) Universal declaration of human rights. In: Yearbook of the United Nations 1948, pp 535–537. New York, Columbia University Press, 1950

Genetral Assembly (1975) Declaration on the protection of all persons being subjected to torture and other cruel, inhuman or degrading treatment or punshment. In: Yearbook of the United Nations 1975, pp 624–625. New York, United Nations, 1978

General Assembly (1989) Resolution 44/29. In: yearbook of the United Nations 1989, pp 828–830. New York, United Nations, 1997
Greenberg KJ, Dratel JI (eds) (2005) The torture papers: The road to Abu Ghraib. Cambridge University Press, New York
Gross ML (2003) Fighting by other means in the mideast: a critical analysis of Israel's assassination policy. Polit Stud 51:350–368
Lekea JK (2003) Missile strike carried out with Yemen Cooperation. J Mil Ethics 2:227–229
Luban David (2005) Liberalism, Torture, and the ticking bomb. VA Law Rev 91:1425–1461
Mell P (2002) Big Brother at the door: balancing National Security with privacy under the USA Patriot Act. Denver Univ Law Rev 80:375–428
Meisels T (2008) The trouble with terror: liberty, security, and the response to terror. Cambridge University Press, Cambridge
Organization of American States (1933) Montevideo convention on the rights and duties of states. Leag Nations Treaty Ser 165:20–43
Posner Eric A, Vermeule Adrian (2006) Emergencies and democratic failure. VA Law Rev 92:1092–1146
Simma B (ed) (2002) The Charter of the United Nations: a commentary, 2nd edn. Oxford University Press, Oxford
Statman D (2004) Targeted killings. Theor Inq Law 5:179–197
Supreme Court (1965) Griswold v. Connecticut. 381 U.S. 479
Supreme Court (1971) Bodie v. Connecticut. 401 U.S. 371
Supreme Court (2004a) Hamdi v. Rumsfeld. 542 U.S. 507
Supreme Court (2004b) Rumsfeld v. Padilla. 542 U.S. 426
Supreme Court (2006) Hamdan v. Rumsfeld. 548 U.S. 557
United Nations (1945) Charter of the United Nations. 1 UNTS (XVI)
United Nations (1949) Geneva Convention (III) Rekative to the Treatment of Prisonerts of War. 75 UNTS 135
United Nations (1966a) International covenant on economic, social and cultural rights. 999 UNTS 3
United Nations (1966b) International covenant on civil and political rights. 999 UNTS 171
United Nations (1984) Convention against Torture and Other Cruel, Inhuman and Degrading Treatment r Punishment. 1465 UNTS 85
United States (1968) Omnibus Crime and Safe Streets Act. 42 USC.Section 3711
United States (1978) Foreign intelligence surveillance Act. 50 USC Chapter 36
United States (2002) Military Commission Order No. 1. DoD MCO No.1, Mar 21 2002
Wellman C (2011) The moral dimensions of human rights. Oxford University Press, Oxford
Wildhaber L (2000) Rotaru v. Romania. (28341/95) ECHR 191

Chapter 6
Moral Limits on State Action

Abstract Some moral philosophers argue that the moral limits on state action are different from and less stringent than those on the actions of private persons. Stanley Benn points out that the interests of the public are of greater magnitude than those of any individual or small group of individuals, that statesmen have a special duty as trustees of the national interests, and that they must act in a jungle world of threatening violence. Thomas Nagel argues that in the public morality consequences of action count more than restrictions on the means used, but in private morality the obligation to respect human rights of other persons outweighs the value of the outcome of action. However, these considerations do not eliminate the relevance of ordinary moral limits on the actions of public officials; they merely add other morally relevant considerations. One should distinguish between a supreme emergency as a threat so great as to be immeasurable against the moral limits on state responses and an almost supreme emergency where the threat so clearly outweighs those limits that there is no need to measure them against one another. The former might make moral limits on state action irrelevant because a necessary condition of morality is some level of security, but the latter would almost never justify any but a limited state response. Although in theory it might be possible for a nation state to be released from the moral obligations that limit measures of counterterrorism, this is highly improbable under any foreseeable conditions in the real world.

State responses to terrorism are by and large more important than international responses, both because nation states have more power than international institutions and because international responses are typically implemented by means of state action. Unfortunately, state responses to terrorism are doubly problematic. There is serious disagreement about when and why they violate moral obligations that ordinarily limit justified conduct, and at the same time moral philosophers disagree about whether or how the ordinary standards of morality determine the justifiability of state action. The previous chapter concluded that there are important moral limits on state responses to terrorism; this chapter will examine the relevance of these moral limits to the actions of nation states.

C. Wellman, *Terrorism and Counterterrorism*, SpringerBriefs in Law 9,
DOI: 10.1007/978-94-007-6007-3_6, © The Author(s) 2013

6.1 Public Morality

There is a Machiavellian tradition in political theory that would challenge the reasoning of the previous chapter on the ground that it fails to recognize the difference between the way in which moral standards apply to private individuals and to public officials. Specifically, the moral obligations that stringently limit individual conduct do not apply to state action without significant qualification. Stanley Benn and Thomas Nagel have recently presented similar explanations of why public morality is different from private morality.

After rejecting the view that Machiavelli is announcing that politics is an activity to which moral judgments do not apply, Stanley Benn suggests: "It seems much more likely that Machiavelli is asserting that the requirements of political life impose special demands which are not merely different from those of private life, but which oppose and override them" (Benn 1983, p. 160). But what makes politics special? For one thing, the interests of the public are presumably of greater magnitude than those of any individual or small group of individuals and therefore more often justify sacrificing a moral principle (Benn 1983, pp. 163–164). For another, although a statesman has a duty to strive to create the conditions for international order, that duty could never override his duty as trustee of the national interest (Benn 1983, p. 165). Finally, the conditions of public life are less well-structured by dependable practices than family life or civil society (Benn 1983, p. 165). Thus:

> I have argued, then, that states and their agents are licensed, in liberal theory, to set aside moral principles for the sake of good outcomes (or, more usually, to avoid bad ones), and that the reason for this is that they are the champions and trustees of the public in a jungle world (Benn 1983, p. 167).

If Benn is correct, then the moral obligations not to harm persons and not to violate their human rights, although genuine, often may not limit morally justified state action.

Thomas Nagel defends a similar view of the relation between moral restrictions and good consequences in public morality. First, "Whoever takes on a public or official role assumes the obligation to serve a special function and often the interests of a special group. Like more personal obligations, this limits the claim that other sorts of reasons can make on him" (Nagel 1978, p. 80). Insofar as public obligations are like private ones, this does not imply that individuals in public roles are released from the moral requirements on the treatment of others (Nagel 1978, p. 81). However, public obligations differ significantly from private obligations because of the way in which moral theory applies to the public institutions that create public roles.

> Two types of concern determine the content of morality: concern with what will happen and concern with what one is doing. Insofar as principles of conduct are determined by the first concern, they will be outcome-oriented or consequentialist, requiring that we promote the best results. Insofar as they are determined by the second, the influence of consequences will be limited by certain restrictions on the means to be used, and also by loosening the requirement that one always pursue the best results. The action-centered aspects of morality include bars against treating people in certain ways that violate their rights... (Nagel 1978, pp. 82–83).

In private life, these two concerns result in a balance that emphasizes restrictions against harming or interfering with others rather than requirements to benefit them, but when applied to public institutions, the same two concerns have a different result because institutions do not have personal lives and they pursue the interests of large numbers of persons. In addition, there is a division of labor in the decision and execution of public action (Nagel 1978, p. 83). Hence, in public morality some of the agent-centered restrictions on means will be weaker than in private morality, and states can legitimately favor their own citizens, although not at any cost whatsoever to non-nationals. And public morality will differ from private morality in according outcomes greater weight (Nagel 1978, p. 84).

Benn and Nagel have identified a number of reasons why public morality differs from private morality. How is each of these relevant to the moral limits on state action? Well, what is state action? It is the action of individuals acting in their official capacities, for example an FBI agent conducting surveillance of someone suspected of supporting a terrorist organization, a soldier capturing a member of the Taliban or a judge ruling on whether a detainee has a right to habeas corpus. It consists in state agents acting in their roles within specialized public institutions. Hence (1) state agents have special moral obligations derived from their public roles. As Nagel observes: "In a rigidly defined role like that of a soldier or judge or prison guard, only a very restricted set of considerations is supposed to bear on what one decides to do, and nearly all general considerations are excluded" (Nagel 1978, p. 80). Perhaps, then, the moral limits described in the previous chapter are irrelevant to state action.

Many moral reasons may not be relevant to the actions of individuals insofar as they are acting in their public roles. Thus, a soldier ordered to capture members of the Taliban has an obligation as a soldier to do so, even if the Taliban is a morally justified organization, and a judge has an obligation as a judge to apply the law regarding any restrictions on the right to habeas corpus even if the relevant law is unjust. Nevertheless, Nagel correctly adds that: "One cannot, by joining the army, undertake an obligation to obey any order whatsoever from one's commanding officer. It is not possible to acquire an obligation to kill indebted gamblers by signing a contract as a mafia hit man" (Nagel 1978, p. 80). This is because the social institutions that create special role obligations are themselves subject to moral assessment.

What, then, determines the morality of the public institutions that constitute a nation state? Perhaps (2) the moral standard of state institutions is the public interest. After rejecting two concepts of politics, A. J. M. Milne proposes:

> Let us try instead thinking of government as the activity of identifying and promoting the public interest at home and the national interest abroad. My thesis, which I shall try to defend in the rest of this essay, is that when properly understood, this idea is the rational basis of both government and politics (Milne 1972, p. 40).

This suggests that states and their institutions are justified by their promotion of the public interest broadly conceived and morally limited only by their failure to do so.

The public interest does seem morally relevant to justified state action in a variety of ways. Nagel asserts that one reason why public morality sometimes justifies sacrificing moral restrictions for the sake of consequences is that: "Public institutions are designed to serve purposes larger than those of particular individuals or families. They tend to pursue the interests of masses of people..." (Nagel 1978, p. 83). And Benn notes one way in which the public interest limits justified state action. "But...whatever the statesman's duty to strive to create the conditions for international order, that duty could never override his duty as trustee of the national interest" (Benn 1983, p. 165). Still, the morality of state institutions and the roles they create cannot be completely explained in terms of the public interest, however broadly conceived.

Milne distinguishes between the public interest at home and the national interest abroad and suggests that only these are relevant to any government. But does this imply that public officials are morally permitted, perhaps even required, to disregard the interests of the rest of humanity? That an action would harm anyone is a moral reason why one ought not to perform it, and that an institution would tend to harm human beings is similarly a reason why it ought not to be created and maintained. The fact that the potential victims are not members of one's own nation state does not eliminate the moral relevance of harm.

Nevertheless, political philosophers often assume that this fact does greatly reduce the moral obligation of state officials to prevent harm. It is true that state institutions do and probably ought to favor the public interest over the international interest. But how could this be morally justified? Nagel justifies sacrificing moral restrictions in public morality because public institutions are designed to serve purposes larger than those of individuals or smaller groups. But surely the interests of all humanity outweigh the interests of the citizens of any single state. Benn asserts that a statesman's duty to the international order could never override his duty as a trustee of the national interest. Now state institutions do impose role obligations to promote the public interest. But it is a mistake to infer that these obligations eliminate or even reduce the moral obligation not to harm non-nationals. Instead, these public roles add a social duty that increases the obligations to avoid harming citizens and to promote the public interest.

But what is the moral justification for state institutions that favor the interests of nationals over those of non-nationals? More fundamentally, why ought the international order to be constituted by sovereign nation states? The short answer is that no more effective system for protecting large numbers of human beings from serious harms and preventing the violation of their human rights is now available. Although a world government might be a moral ideal, international relations today and perhaps human nature forever make that impracticable.

A nation state is morally legitimate only if it protects its citizens from harm and prevents the violation of their human rights. Its constituting institutions are morally justified only if they also tend to prevent harm to non-nationals and to respect their human rights. Thus it is a mistake, or at least misleading, to suggest that the moral standard of state institutions is simply the public interest or even the interests of all humanity. State institutions ought also to be constituted in such a way that they will protect human rights. Although moral human rights are presumably grounded upon the interests of human beings in some way, many of them have a political urgency that makes them focal points in any moral assessment of nation states.

Stanley Benn advances another reason why public morality differs from the morality of private action. (3) Nation states act in a jungle world. Because of the absence of effective international institutions to protect human beings from harm and prevent the violation of their human rights, state action is conducted under conditions of vastly greater risk than are the actions of individual persons acting within the relatively secure environment of their nation state. Although this state of insecurity may fall short of a Hobbesian state of nature, it is serious enough to impose special moral requirements upon state action.

A private individual is morally permitted to expose her interests to a considerable degree of risk and to entrust the security of her human rights primarily to others. But a nation state and its officials act as trustees of the basic interests and human rights of its citizens. This fiduciary relationship imposes a duty to act for the benefit of its nationals and especially not to expose their interests and human rights to unnecessary risk. It also imposes a secondary duty to maintain the conditions that enable it to act effectively to protect the public from serious harms or the violation of their human rights.

However, Benn significantly exaggerates the moral force of this consideration when he concludes:

> I have argued, then, that states and their agents are licensed, in liberal theory, to set aside moral principles for the sake of good outcomes (or, more usually, to avoid bad ones), and that the reason for this is that they are the champions and trustees of the public in a jungle world (Benn 1983, p. 167).

The state's moral obligation to avoid any unnecessary risk of bad outcomes for its citizens does not permit it or its agents to set aside the ordinary moral limitations on state action. It merely qualifies the applicability of these limits in a manner that makes them less strict under conditions of high risk to the interests and rights of its public.

Accordingly, there is a public morality of state action that is significantly different from the ordinary morality of private conduct for three reasons. State agents have special obligations derived from their roles in the social institutions that constitute the nation state. These obligations permit and even require state officials to favor their own citizens, even though the social institutions from which they are derived are morally justified in part by their tendency to protect the basic interests and human rights of all human beings. And third, state agents act under conditions of greater risk than do private persons rendered relatively secure by the institutions of their own states. Nevertheless, this public morality neither excludes nor reduces the ordinary moral limits on action, the duties not to harm any human being and not to violate the human rights of any individual. Rather, it adds a moral obligation of public officials to serve the interests and protect the rights of the members of their nation state that modifies the applicability of the ordinary limits on the moral permissibility of action.

6.2 Supreme Emergency

One especially high risk that has received considerable attention in the literature is a supreme emergency. On the 19th of May 1940 in his first BBC broadcast to the nation, Winston Churchill reported that the Germans had broken through the French defenses north of the Maginot Line and ravaged the open country beyond. He then declared:

> Our task is not only to win the battle—but to win the war. After this battle in France abates its force, there will come the battle for our Island—for all that Britain is, and all that Britain means. That will be the struggle. In that supreme emergency we shall not hesitate to take every step, even the most drastic, to call forth from our people the last ounce and the last inch of effort of which they are capable.

Michael Walzer recognizes that Churchill's description of Britain's predicament as a "supreme emergency" was a rhetorical gesture, but he suggests that implicit in it is the moral argument that there could be a danger so extreme that it justifies measures absolutely prohibited by the international war convention (Walzer 1977, p. 251).

This is a plausible but obscure argument. What could such a supreme emergency be? I am not asking the merely scholarly question of how Walzer uses the phrase "a supreme emergency" in his publications. I am seeking the moral insight implicit in his argument to justify violations of the war convention. That is, how should one define the concept of a supreme emergency in order to explain its moral force?

One might well begin with Walzer's observation that a supreme emergency is best understood in terms of necessity.

> Though its use is often ideological, the meaning of the phrase is a matter of common sense. It is defined by two criteria which correspond to the two levels on which the concept of necessity works: the first has to do with the imminence of the danger and the second with its nature. The two criteria must be applied. Neither one by itself is sufficient as an account of extremity or as a defense of the extraordinary measures extremity is thought to require (Walzer 1977, p. 252).

Thus, a supreme emergency justifies measures that are ordinarily morally wrong because extraordinary measures are necessary to prevent the extreme danger it threatens.

The criterion of imminence might be misleading. The *Oxford English Dictionary* defines "imminent" as "Of an event, esp. danger or disaster: impending, soon to happen." But how soon? A German victory, Walzer's paradigm example of a supreme emergency, was not possible in the immediate future at the time when the decision to bomb German cities was taken. What was necessary was immediate action, action without delay, to prevent the victory that otherwise was so certain. Thus, Walzer's first criterion is best interpreted as the need for immediate action to prevent a certain or almost certain disaster.

His second criterion, the nature of the danger, is much more difficult to interpret. What kind of a danger could constitute a supreme emergency? Walzer tells us that "If we are to adopt or defend the adoption of extreme measures, the danger must be of an unusual and horrifying kind" (Walzer 1977, p. 253). This description does not carry its meaning on its sleeve. Let us begin by exploring the idea of a horrifying danger. To be horrifying is to cause horror, and the OED defines horror as "(A painful feeling of) intense loathing and fear; a terrified and revolted shuddering; a strong aversion or an intense dislike (of); *colloq.* dismay (at)." In the same paragraph Walzer writes "For Nazism lies at the outer limits of exigency, at a point where we are likely to find ourselves united in fear and abhorrence." And the OED defines the transitive verb "abhor" as "Regard with disgust and hatred." Now one can understand how danger, especially an extreme danger, would incite fear, but it is hard to imagine how fearfulness would justify measures that the war convention bans. On the other hand, the fact that a danger is horrifying or abhorrent might justify measures that are normally immoral if, but only if, the danger is of the sort that would cause moral horror or aversion in any morally sensitive person. I do not know whether Walzer intends his reader to interpret his psychological descriptions to refer to specifically moral emotions, but I suggest that this is required if they are to point to any moral justification. To my mind, the Preface of the *Universal Declaration of Human Rights,* also mindful of the Nazi atrocities, makes the point much more clearly when it reports: "*Whereas* disregard and contempt for human rights have resulted in barbarous acts which have outraged the conscience of mankind…" (General Assembly 1948, p. 535).

Walzer insists that a supreme emergency must also be unusual. But what could the abnormality of the danger have to do with its supremacy? My guess is that the clue is implicit in Walzer's mathematical descriptions. He explains why the danger of a Nazi victory constitutes an extreme emergency by asserting that "the consequences of a final victory were literally beyond calculation, immeasurably awful" (Walzer 1977, p. 253). And the subtitle of the last section of this chapter is "The Limits of Calculation." Thus, an extreme danger has consequences so immense that their moral disvalue cannot be compared with the moral disvalue of any extraordinary measures that could be taken to avert them. Well, how does one compare moral values and disvalues when making a morally responsible decision? It is, for example, by weighing the importance of the harms caused and rights violated against the importance of the harms prevented and the rights protected. And a morally mature person is able to make such difficult judgments because of his or her experience of moral deliberation and the retrospective reevaluation of moral decisions of oneself and others. But past experience becomes irrelevant when the moral danger at stake is so great that one has no sense of exactly how to balance its disvalue against the values at stake under normal circumstances. All one can know is that it is greatly disproportionate, but by an amount off the scales of the normal balancing of moral values. It is in this respect, and only in this way, that an extreme emergency must be unusual.

Walzer's argument hinges on a single example of a supreme emergency, a German victory in the Second World War. He regards this as a general danger to every country in Europe and perhaps to all mankind. He then asks: "Can a supreme emergency be constituted by a particular threat—by a threat of enslavement or extermination directed against a single nation?" (Walzer 1977, p. 254). With considerable hesitation, he replies in the affirmative. He suggests that the survival and freedom of political communities are the highest values of the international society and asserts: "Nazism challenged these values on a grand scale, but challenges more narrowly conceived, *if they are of the same kind*, have similar moral consequences. They bring us under the rule of necessity (and necessity knows no rules)" (Walzer 1977, p. 254). I would agree without hesitation. Surely the threat of the enslavement or extermination of the people of a single nation would constitute a supreme emergency, an unusual and horrifying danger as I have interpreted this definition.

Could terrorism ever constitute a supreme emergency? Although Walzer's argument concerns only the justification of state actions that violate the war convention, there is nothing in the concept of a supreme emergency to limit it to the morality of warfare. If a supreme emergency really could override the moral limits on just wars, presumably it could for the same reasons override other restrictions on morally permissible state action. Among these might be the moral limits on state responses to terrorism.

Did the terrorist attack on 9/11 constitute a supreme emergency? If so, would it have justified shooting down the two planes high-jacked by terrorists had the United States Air Force known of this terrorist attack? How, if at all, could one balance on the moral scales the killing of many innocent passengers and airline personnel against the threat to the lives of an indefinite number of persons in the Twin Towers? In comparison, the ticking bomb scenario seems much less controversial. David Luban describes this situation as follows:

> Suppose the bomb is planted somewhere in the crowded heart of an American city, and you have custody of the man who planted it. He won't talk. Surely, the hypothetical suggests, we shouldn't be too squeamish to torture the information out of him and save hundreds of lives. Consequences count, and strict moral prohibitions must yield to the calculus of consequences (Luban 2005, p. 1440).

This does seem like a clear case of an extreme emergency, although it is an imaginary and merely hypothetical rather than a real-life situation. Or suppose, as is realistically possible, that some terrorist organization were to acquire a nuclear device and threaten to detonate it in the center of a heavily populated metropolitan area. Would this be an extreme emergency sufficient to justify extraordinary measures of a kind that would be grossly immoral under normal circumstances? I believe these examples show that an extraordinary terrorist threat could constitute a supreme emergency. However, they also show that none or almost none of the terrorist threats nation states actually face pose the immeasurable degree of moral danger required for a genuine supreme emergency.

What, then, can one learn about the moral limits on state action under realistic circumstances from an examination of Walzer's reasoning about supreme emergencies? Emergencies by their very nature are dangerous situations; they threaten serious harm, often disaster. Hence, they create fear that motivates public officials to respond with immoral actions and that motivates citizens to call for and support such responses. As Walzer observes, "Fear and hysteria are always latent in combat, often real, and they press us toward fearful measures and criminal behavior" (Walzer 1977, p. 251). Even if the war against terrorism is not, strictly speaking, one kind of war, it is certainly a form of combat against fearful dangers.

Absolute or near absolute prohibitions against immoral responses to terrorism are needed in international conventions and national legislation to counteract the extreme fear that terrorism arouses. Similarly, "The war convention is a bar to such measures, not always effective, but there nevertheless. In principle, at least, as we have seen, it resists the ordinary crises of military life" (Walzer 1977, p. 251). Without very strong prohibitions in national and international law, state officials would much more often respond to extreme public anxiety by engaging in counter-terrorism actions that cannot be justified morally.

State officials typically attempt to justify their responses to terrorism by a cost-benefit analysis, for example by insisting that the costs to innocent persons detained or terrorist suspects denied due process are much less than the benefits of preventing the death of innocent citizens or damage to their property. Walzer rejects this sort of act-utilitarian justification.

> The problem is that it is too easy to juggle the figures. Utilitarianism, which was supposed to be the most precise and hard-headed of moral arguments, turns out to be speculative and arbitrary. For we have to assign values where there is no agreed valuation, no recognized hierarchy of value, no market mechanism for determining the positive or negative worth of different acts and outcomes (Walzer 2004, p. 38).

He adds that "Commonly, what we are calculating is *our* benefit (which we exaggerate) and *their* cost (which we minimize or disregard entirely)" (Walzer 2004, p. 39). Although this is in part a merely pragmatic criticism based on our psychological biases, it is also a deeper theoretical objection. Because one cannot define any units by which to measure specifically moral value, one cannot calculate the overall moral value or disvalue of any state response to terrorism.

Although it might be possible to make a moderately reliable estimate of the amount of harm caused versus the amount of harm prevented by a controversial state response to terrorism, there is no comparable version of what Robert Nozick calls a "utilitarianism of rights" (Nozick 1974, p. 28). Walzer asserts that: "It is the acknowledgement of rights that puts a stop to such calculations and forces us to realize that the destruction of the innocent, whatever its purposes, is a kind of blasphemy against our deepest moral commitments" (Walzer 1977, p. 262). He is correct to insist that our commitment to the protection of human rights is deeper than our commitment to the prevention of harm, but he exaggerates when he insists that the absolutism of rights is a shield that defends the innocent and is impenetrable to moral argument (Walzer 2004, p. 35). Although moral rights, and especially fundamental human rights, impose very strong moral limits on permissible state responses to terrorism, these limits are not absolute. Not only is it sometimes morally permissible to violate the rights of some human beings in order to protect the rights of others, it is sometimes permissible to violate even a human right to prevent a vast amount of harm to innocent persons. Still, because human rights do weigh especially heavily in the moral scales, they do impose very strong limits on morally permissible state action.

These moral limits are never suspended, not even in a supreme emergency. Thus, Walzer maintains:

> There are no moments in human history that are not governed by moral rules; the human world is a world of limitation, and moral limits are never suspended—the way we might, for example, suspend *habeas corpus* in a time of civil war. But there are moments when the rules can be and perhaps have to be overridden. They have to be overridden precisely because they have not been suspended (Walzer 2004, p. 34).

No matter what the circumstances, state officials and private individuals always have a moral obligation not to harm any human being and not to violate a human right of any person. Therefore, there are always strong moral limits on state responses to terrorism. Nevertheless, very strongest moral prohibitions can sometimes be overridden.

> The evil of Nazism suggests the positive form of the supreme-emergency argument. It is that sort of evil, uncommon even in the long history of human violence, that pushes us beyond rights normality…. And if we can see clearly, with the help of such an example, when the normal defense of rights can be overridden, we can also see clearly why it can't be overridden short of that (Walzer 2004, p. 47).

But if one rejects Walzer's assumption that rights are absolute, as I do, then one must ask whether the moral limits they impose on state responses to terrorism can be overridden short of an extreme emergency.

If so, it would have to be an almost supreme emergency. But what could constitute an almost supreme emergency? Well I have defined a supreme emergency as an imminent danger that is morally horrifying and "unusual" in the sense of being so greatly evil as to be off the scales of any normal balancing of moral values. At this point Walzer gives us a relevant insight.

> "Supreme emergency" describes those rare moments when the negative value that we assign—that we cannot help assigning—to the disaster that looms before us disvalues morality itself and leaves us free to do whatever is militarily necessary to avoid the disaster, so long as what we do doesn't produce an even worse disaster (Walzer 2004, p. 40).

Thus, there is a moral limit of proportionality even in the ethics of supreme emergency. Hence, I suggest that just as a supreme emergency can override the normal limits on some state action because it consists of a moral danger so abnormally great as to be disproportionate to a state response to terrorism in a way that makes it immeasurable in the sense of being incapable of being weighed by the normal balancing of moral values, so an almost extreme emergency can override the normal limits on state action when the moral harms the emergency would inflict are so very disproportionate that although they can be balanced against the moral harms the state action would inflict, the former so clearly outweigh the latter that the moral permissibly of state action cannot be subject to any reasonable doubt. Presumably this sort of moral justification is sometimes, although rarely, applicable to state responses to terrorism under realistic circumstances.

6.3 Release from Moral Obligations

The moral limits on state responses to terrorism consist of moral duties that oblige a nation state not to take certain kinds of action. The most obvious example is the moral duty not to cause unnecessary, avoidable and disproportionate, harm to human beings or their property. But in practice the most important and most controversial moral limits are moral obligations imposed by human rights that might be and sometimes are violated by state responses to terrorism. Thus, surveillance is limited by the human right to privacy, detention by the human right to liberty, interrogation by the human right not to be tortured, and trials by the human right to due process. These rights limit state action by imposing moral duties not to invade the privacy of any individual, not to detain anyone by force, not to torture any human being and not to deny due process to anyone on trial before a court or tribunal.

The moral limits on state responses to terrorism are never suspended, not even in a supreme emergency. These moral duties are general; that is they impose prima facie moral obligations not to act in specific ways whatever the circumstances. But because they are prima facie rather than absolute, they are not always morally binding. Therefore, state officials are sometimes released from one or more of their moral obligations not to respond to terrorism in ways that are ordinarily morally wrong. What, then, can release one from some normally binding moral obligation?

(1) An overriding moral reason can sometimes release one from one's moral obligation. Moral obligations are grounded upon duty-imposing moral reasons. These are dual-aspect practical reasons, reasons both for a moral agent to act or refrain from acting in some manner and for those in society with an agent to react negatively in the event that he or she acts contrary to this reason (Wellman 1995, pp. 43–50). But a duty-imposing moral reason may, under some circumstances, be outweighed by a more stringent contrary duty-imposing reason. In any such case, the agent is not morally obligated to perform the action that would otherwise be morally obligatory.

For example, the individual's human right to liberty imposes a prima facie moral obligation upon all state agents not to detain anyone by force. However, this duty may sometimes be overridden by the contrary moral obligation of state officials to protect the members of their society from serious harm or the violation of their human rights. Thus, it will sometimes be morally permissible to detain someone briefly if there is evidence that he or she is about to engage in terrorism against the state. In such a case, the state official is released from the moral obligation not to detain by force by the necessity of detention in order to fulfill the contrary and more stringent state obligation to protect its nationals. However, detention must be strictly necessary, not merely convenient. If there were some less morally objectionable means of preventing the individual from engaging in terrorism, then the moral obligation not to detain by force would not be overridden.

Similarly, the individual's human right to privacy imposes a moral obligation upon public officials not to require a bank or credit card company to secretly reveal the bank records or credit card account of any person suspected of giving financial aid to some terrorist organization or group. However, this state obligation may be overridden by the contrary state obligation to protect its citizens from terrorism. This may well be the case because accessing the financial records of an individual is a relatively modest invasion of the right to privacy, provided that the information gained remains confidential to those public officials with an urgent need to know it, and the terrorist organization or group poses a serious threat and depends for its activities upon financial assistance from this individual. However, the state's moral obligation to respect the individual's human right to privacy may be limited by its contrary moral obligation to protect its residents in this case only because its action is a relatively unimportant invasion of privacy and the potential threat to its residents relatively serious. A principle of proportionality is presupposed when a moral obligation is overridden by a conflicting moral obligation; the latter must be relatively strong and the former relatively weak given the circumstances. And because the stringency of a moral obligation varies with the circumstances, there is no generally applicable hierarchy of moral obligations.

Finally, the individual's human right to due process imposes upon public officials a moral obligation not to deny due process to any individual it charges with one or more illegal acts. But it might be morally permissible to deny the right to cross examine a witness of the prosecution when this is necessary to avoid revealing the identity of an under-cover agent of the police or an anti-terrorism state agency. In such a case, the moral obligation to provide due process would be limited by the secondary moral obligation to preserve the efficiency of the state's counter-terrorism agencies needed to fulfill its primary moral obligation to protect its citizens. Presumably, the state's moral obligation to respect all the other due process rights of the individual would remain unqualified by this very restricted release from moral obligation.

(2) A canceling action can release one from a moral obligation. Everyone has a human right to personal security that imposes a number of moral obligations including the duty not to batter or even strike another person. However, one can cancel this duty regarding a second party by consenting to participate in a manly sport because by consenting one is waiving one's right to personal security against one's opponent. For example, if a friend challenges one to a boxing match, one can accept the challenge by saying "yes, let's box." As a consequence, one's friend does not violate any moral duty not to strike or batter one even if he manages to hit one with considerable force and even give one a black eye or bloody nose, at least if he or she respects the rules of manly sports.

Terrorism is not a sport, but one can imagine situations in which a person might cancel, at least in part, a moral obligation that normally limits state responses. I have visited Iran three times in the past few years to participate in conferences organized by the Center for the Study of Human Rights at Mofid University in Qom. And I often review papers submitted for presentation at these conferences as well as serving more generally as advisor to this center. Imagine that the United

States government learns of my visits and, being suspicious of any alleged concern for human rights in the city where the majority of Imams are educated, asks to have access to all e-mail messages I receive from or send to Iran. Confident in my innocence and that of my Iranian colleagues, I might well give my consent, thereby waiving my human right to privacy in that matter and partially canceling the duty of federal agent not to invade the privacy of my correspondence.

Or imagine that a professor of comparative religions with a special interest in religious education travels to Pakistan to study Islamic educational institutions. In addition to visiting public universities, she spends several days observing teaching methods in a large madraseh. Unbeknownst to her, this madraseh is alleged to have participated in the training of several terrorists. Upon her return to the United States, she is charged with cooperation with a terrorist organization. Intent on minimizing procedural barriers, the government chooses to bypass the federal courts and submit her case to a military tribunal. Although as a United States citizen she could insist upon her right to be tried in a court that would more fully respect her due process rights, she might consent to be tried before a military tribunal because she believes, on the advice of her lawyer, that in that forum she can more quickly clear her name. If she does give her consent, then she has in effect waived part of her human right to due process and in part cancelled the state's moral obligation to provide due process in her trial.

Although the stories I have told illustrate one way in which a moral obligation can be canceled, they are rather far-fetched. This suggests that nation states will very seldom if ever be released from the normal limits on state responses to terrorism in this manner. Hence, a state might attempt to cancel some limiting obligation by declaring a state of emergency. Public officials could cite Article 4.1 of the *International Covenant on Civil and Political Rights* that reads in part:

> In time of emergency which threatens the life of the nation and the existence of which is officially proclaimed, the States Parties to the present covenant may take measures derogating from their obligations under the present Covenant to the extent strictly required by the exigencies of the situation… (United Nations 1966).

Although any such state action would cancel the state's obligations to respect in full the human rights to liberty, personal security and privacy conferred by international law, it would leave its moral obligations imposed by the corresponding moral human rights untouched. Moral human rights are, in the language of the French *Declaration of the Rights of Man and the Citizen*, imprescriptible (France 1789, p. 8). That is, they cannot be suspended or extinguished by any state action. This is because no action that public officials could possibly take would eliminate or even reduce the grounds of these non-institutional human rights (Wellman 1997, pp. 248–254). Therefore, the moral obligations they impose on state responses to terrorism cannot be cancelled by the state in any way or to the slightest degree.

Can a moral obligation that would normally limit state responses be canceled by the forfeiture of the duty-imposing moral human right? If so, then public officials might be justified in taking extreme measures against terrorists or those who support terrorism. Many political leaders and some moral philosophers believe that by causing dreadful harms to innocent victims and grossly violating their human rights terrorists forfeit their own moral human rights. However, this cannot be true. One does not need to earn one's moral human rights, nor are one's human rights contingent upon good behavior. What qualifies anyone for the possession of moral human rights is simply the fact that one is a human being in the morally relevant sense. This is one's nature as an individual that is a member of the biological species of human beings with the psychological capacities necessary for moral agency. One does not cease to be a human being even when one acts in a most inhumane way. Therefore, the moral obligations of a nation state to respect the moral human rights of all those affected by its responses to terrorism are never canceled by forfeiture.

(3) The absence of a necessary condition for moral obligation in general can sometimes release one from a specific moral obligation. One necessary condition for moral obligation is that one will not suffer excessive sacrifice by doing one's duty. J. O. Urmson provides an illuminating example of an act over and beyond the call of duty for this reason:

> We may imagine a squad of soldiers to be practicing the throwing of hand grenades; a grenade slips from the hand of one of them and rolls on the ground near the squad; one of them sacrifices his life by throwing himself on the grenade and protecting his comrades with his own body. It is quite unreasonable to suppose that such a man must be impelled by the sort of emotion that he might be impelled by if his best friend were in the squad; he might only just have joined the squad; it is clearly an action having moral status. But if the soldier had not thrown himself on the grenade would he have failed in his duty? (Urmson 1958, p. 202).

Clearly the answer to this rhetorical question is in the negative.

But why would insisting that the soldier has a moral obligation to sacrifice himself for the sake of his comrades be demanding that he make an excessive sacrifice? It might seem that sacrificing one life to save several lives would be required by practical reason. This would be true if the relevant measure were a cost benefit analysis, but what makes a sacrifice excessive in the sense that releases one from moral obligation is not that the harm incurred outweighs the beneficial consequences of one's action. What is relevant is that the sacrifice is intolerable, that no normal moral agent could accept it. This is a specific application of the Kantian principle that "ought" implies "can." That is, one has a moral obligation to perform some action only if it is possible for one to do so.

At first glance, and even upon some reflection, this Kantian principle seems inapplicable to the example cited above. Surely, the fact that this soldier did sacrifice his life for his comrades shows that it was possible for him to do so. This is true. But in sacrificing his very life this soldier did something that it would be psychologically impossible for most moral agents to do. The relevant standard of psychological impossibility is objective rather than subjective, general rather than individual. Otherwise, weakness of will would release an individual from all but the least demanding obligations. But why not hold each individual morally responsible for acting as he or she is capable of doing? The explanation lies in the nature of duty-imposing reasons as dual-aspect practical reasons, reasons both for an agent to act or refrain from acting in some manner and for those in society with that agent to react negatively in the event that he or she fails to do so. Now in the example cited, the reason for the soldier to sacrifice his life, to save the lives of his comrades, is not eliminated or reduced by the psychological inability of the normal agent to so act. However, the reason for those in society with the soldier to react negatively is eliminated or reduced. A duty-imposing reason is a reason for others to react negatively because the fact that an agent refuses or fails to act on it normally shows the agent to have personality traits, such as selfishness or malice, that tend to damage or destroy interpersonal relationships. But these character traits are general dispositions to act or refrain from acting in some manner in most cases, usually under normal circumstances. Therefore, in failing to make a sacrifice that most moral agents would be incapable of making, an agent has not shown any character traits contrary to sociability.

Could excessive sacrifice ever release public officials from the moral limits on state action? Michael Walzer suggests by implication that it might. In criticism of Prime Minister Baldwin's justification of terror bombing as inevitable, he writes:

> But the argument is wrong at both ends. It is simply not the case that individuals will always strike out at innocent men and women rather than accept risks for themselves. We even say, very often, that it is their duty to accept risks (and perhaps to die); and here as in moral life generally, "ought" implies "can." We make the demand knowing that it is possible for people to live up to it. Can we make the same demand on political leaders, acting not for themselves but for their countrymen? That will depend upon the dangers their countrymen face (Walzer 1977, p. 252).

Presumably he has a supreme emergency in mind here.

To my mind, something less than a supreme emergency might, conceivably might, release a public official from the normal moral limits on state responses by virtue of excessive sacrifice. Suppose that a public official has in custody someone who probably has information that the state could use to prevent a monstrous terrorist attack. If the suspect refuses to divulge this information, the public official might find the urge to extract it by torture irresistible. Or imagine that a charismatic leader of a highly dangerous group of terrorists has been detained for questioning. It seems imperative that he be convicted of criminal activity in order to prevent him from recruiting additional members to his group and instigating new and even more devastating acts of terrorism. Although the evidence of his guilt is conclusive, much of it could not be revealed in a public trial or even in a military tribunal without jeopardizing national security. Even a very conscientious public official might find himself unable to resist infringing the terrorist's human rights to liberty and due process if this is necessary to avoid releasing him. Given the frequency of police brutality when interrogating suspects and the number of cases in which police and district attorneys fail to respect due process rights such as presumption of innocence or full discovery, there may be something in human nature that occasionally makes it psychologically impossible for most public officials to fulfill their normal moral obligations. If so, they would be released from these moral limitations on state action by virtue of intolerable sacrifice.

But the psychology presupposed in these scenarios is highly speculative and the line between hard to resist and irresistible is almost impossible to draw. Therefore, although it is theoretically possible that state officials are sometimes released by excessive sacrifice from their moral obligations to respect fully the human rights of all those affected by their actions, one cannot be confident that this ever actually happens.

A second necessary condition for moral obligation is that it not impose an unreasonable constraint upon the moral agent. Thomas Hobbes describes the state of nature as a war of every man against every man in which the life of man is "solitary, poor, nasty, brutish and short" (Hobbes 1996, pp. 88–89). He maintains that in such a state individuals are released from the moral obligations that would be binding upon them in a state of society.

> The Lawes of Nature oblige *in foro interno*; they bind to a desire that they should take place; but *in foro externo*, that is, to the putting them in act, not always. For he that should be modest, and tractable, and perform all he promises, in such time, and place, where no man else should do so, should but make himself a prey to others, and procure his own certain ruin, contrary to the ground of all Lawes of Nature, which tend to preservation (Hobbes 1996, p. 110).

Thus, the insecurity one would face in a state of nature would release one from all moral obligations.

The words "and procure his own certain ruin" suggest an excessive sacrifice. However, in this passage Hobbes is not presupposing the Kantian principle that "ought" implies "can." What releases individuals from performing their normal moral obligations in a state of nature is not that it would be psychologically impossible for them to do so but that this would be contrary to the ground, the rational justification, of all the laws of nature that impose our moral obligations. Because "A LAW OF NATURE, (*Lex Naturalis*,) is a Precept, or general Rule, found out by Reason…" (Hobbes 1996, p. 91) it could not impose any unreasonable moral obligations. Thus, the Hobbesian principle is that "ought" implies "reasonable." Although I do not agree with Hobbes that moral obligations are imposed by laws of nature, by universal moral principles, I do agree that a moral agent is released from any moral obligation when it would impose an unreasonable constraint. This is because any moral obligation is grounded upon a duty-imposing reason, and it is this grounding reason that constrains a moral agent to act accordingly. Since what obliges, binds or constrains, an agent to act morally is the force of reason, moral obligations hold only as long as this constraint is not contrary to reason.

However, I do not agree with Hobbes that an act is reasonable only if it promotes the agent's self-interest.

> Whensoever a man Transferreth his Right, or Renounceth it; it is either in consideration of some Right reciprocally transferred to himself; or for some other good he hopeth for thereby. For it is a voluntary act; and of the voluntary acts of every man, the object is some *Good to himself* (Hobbes 1996, p. 93).

Here Hobbes assumes that the rational justification of any voluntary action consists in the fact that it is a means to some end and that this end must be something that is of value to the agent because he or she desires it. But what makes some end valuable is that it is desirable, not that it is desired. And it need not be desirable for the agent in order to justify acting to achieve it. That a contribution to charity would benefit others is a reason to contribute, and the fact that one's action would harm another person, even a stranger, is a reason to refrain from so acting. Practical reason is not limited to prudential reasons. Hence, it may be and sometimes is reasonable to perform a moral obligation even at some sacrifice to one's own well-being.

But if acting morally is not necessarily in one's self-interest and may even involve self-sacrifice, why act morally? This is a question that anyone might well ask when finding oneself faced with the choice of whether to fulfill some burdensome moral obligation. What is one asking when, reluctant to make some sacrifice, one asks "why should I do my duty?" One may be asking for an adequate reason to act morally or one may be asking to be motivated to act morally (Prichard 1912, pp. 21–37). Now if "ought" implies "reasonable," then the former is a serious question that calls for an answer. But the answer seems easy. It is simply the duty-imposing moral reason that grounds the moral obligation one is reluctant to fulfill. If, on the other hand, one is asking to be motivated to do one's duty, then it seems to pose no problem for moral philosophy because it presents no challenge to the reasonableness of moral obligation. Thus, by revealing the ambiguity in the question asked, conceptual analysis seems to show that what appears to be a deep and difficult philosophical problem is nothing but mere confusion and no problem at all.

But a problem does remain. Why would a moral agent, someone with the capacity to understand and act on moral reasons, be reluctant to fulfill a reasonable moral obligation? It is because he or she does not appreciate the moral force of the duty-imposing reason in the given situation. The weight of a duty-imposing moral reason depends upon the circumstances. Although, "to do that would harm another person" is always a reason not to perform that action, different kinds of action cause very different kinds of harm and to a greater or lesser extent in different situations. Similarly, "that act would violate someone's human right to privacy" may be a very strong or relatively weak duty-imposing reason depending upon what kind of information is gained, how it is accessed, to whom it is made available, and how it might be used to the detriment of the right-holder. Thus the remaining problem is to explain the strength of duty-imposing reasons in such a way that one can judge their moral force in varying situations. And this is a problem for moral philosophy.

Fortunately, it is a problem that can be postponed for another day. The question that must be addressed for present purposes is whether public officials are ever released from the normal moral limits on state responses to terrorism by their unreasonableness. Some might argue that because there is no international sovereign to secure even their continued existence, nation states are in a state of nature that releases them from any moral obligations they would have were their preservation more secure. However, no such argument is valid. Although there is no global state, there is an international community of states that makes and with some success enforces international law. Moreover, the plausible but false assumption that all moral reasoning is grounded on self-preservation is far less plausible when applied to states than to individuals (Hobbes 1996, p. 90). Nation states are not ends-in-themselves; they are institutions that are instrumentally valuable to the extent that they respect the human rights of individual persons, protect them from serious harms and contribute to their well-being. In the event that one nation state replaces another, the lives of the vast majority of those affected normally go on much as before. Therefore, even a threat to the very existence of a nation state, something that terrorists are almost never capable of delivering, would not release a state from the normal moral limits on its response to terrorism by making performance of these obligations unreasonable.

Accordingly, the moral obligations that limit permissible action by individual persons are equally relevant to the actions of state officials. To be sure, public morality is different from private morality. But it imposes additional moral obligations arising from the institutional responsibilities of public officials rather than canceling or reducing their moral obligations as individual moral agents. Similarly, a supreme emergency or an almost supreme emergency might override the usual moral limits on state action, but neither would eliminate these moral obligations. Although one can imagine situations in which some right-holder might theoretically cancel a limiting moral obligation of public officials, this would very seldom if ever occur in practice. Equally rare would be situations in which a public official is released from some limiting moral obligation because of excessive sacrifice. Finally, it is not true that nation states interact in a state of nature that releases them from any and all moral obligations. Thus, the normal moral limits on state responses to terrorism are always applicable and public officials are released from them primarily if not exclusively only when they are overridden by some more stringent contrary moral obligation.

6.4 An Overview

There is so much controversy about the proper definition of terrorism that some authorities have concluded that no useful definition is possible. But if one is to write or think seriously about terrorism, one needs to identify one's subject-matter. And readers will be unable to judge the adequacy of one's conclusions if they do not know to what they refer. Therefore, I persist in defining terrorism as "the attempt to coerce an indirect target by means of terror produced by the use or threat of violence against a direct target."

However, I do not insist that my definition is the only proper one. The usefulness of a definition depends upon the purposes for which it is used. Since my project is to identify and assess the moral considerations relevant to terrorism, I have defined it in a way that is general enough to cover the paradigm cases of terrorism together with instances that are very similar, but in such a way that I do not prejudge the question of whether terrorism is ever morally justified. Quite different and probably more restricted definitions would be needed to define terrorism as a tort or crime in any national legal system or to define it for the purposes of international law.

Terrorism as I have defined it is never morally innocent. Any attempt to coerce by means of terror produced by the use or threat of violence has four essential wrong-making characteristics. It is coercive; it terrorizes; it uses or threatens violence; and it uses persons as means only. Several species of terrorism have additional wrong-making characteristics. For example, political terrorism undermines trust in a context of mutual dependence and disrupts the patterns of social activity that sustain the social order. State terrorism violates the moral duty of a nation state to protect its population from harm and violates their moral right to equitable treatment under law. Thus terrorism is always prima facie morally wrong, typically very seriously immoral.

Nevertheless, an act of terrorism might be morally justified. It could be justified when the importance of the human rights it protects together with the balance of the resulting benefits and harms outweighs the importance of the human rights it violates together with the harms it creates. A plausible situation in which this might be true is a supreme emergency or almost extreme emergency that might be effectively met only by terrorist activity. However, historical experience suggests that very few actual acts of terrorism can be justified.

As international terrorism has grown in frequency and destructiveness, the international community has responded in increasingly forceful ways, especially sanctions imposed by the Security Council. It has justified its responses as actions necessary to protect the human rights of potential victims and to preserve international peace and friendly relations among nation states. To date, these measures have respected the sovereignty of nation states and the human rights of those affected.

Nation states have political authority, the moral right to make and enforce rules governing all those within its territory, primarily because of the way they protect their subjects from serious harms and especially violations of their human rights. This protection will often require, and thus justify, forceful responses to domestic or international terrorism. However, state responses are justified only when they respect the human rights of all those affected, especially the human rights to privacy, liberty, due process and not to be tortured. Unfortunately, some of the recent responses of the United States and the United Kingdom have violated one or more of these human rights in an unjustifiable manner.

Public morality, the moral considerations relevant to the actions of public officials, is very different from the morality of private agents. However, it does not eliminate any of the normal moral limits on justifiable action. Rather, it adds special obligations to serve the interests and protect the rights of the members of the nation state, obligations that sometimes modify the normal limits on permissible action. This is illustrated most dramatically in a supreme or almost supreme emergency that might provide an overriding moral obligation that releases public officials from the usual moral limitations on justified action. Although public officials could in theory be released from limiting obligations by some canceling action or undue sacrifice, this is highly unlikely in any realistic scenario.

References

Benn, SI (1983) Private and public morality: clean living and dirty hands. In: SI Benn, GF Gaus (eds) Public and private in social life, pp. 155–181. Croom Helm, London and St. Martin's Press, New York

France (1789) Declaration of the rights of man and of the citizen. In: Brownlie I (eds) Basic documents on human rights, 1st edn. Clarendon Press, Oxford, pp. 8–10, 1971

General Assembly (1948) Universal declaration of human rights. In: Yearbook of the United Nations 1948. Columbia University Press, New York, pp. 535–537

Hobbes T (1996) In: Tuck R (ed) Leviathan. Cambridge University Press, Cambridge

Luban D (2005) Liberalism, torture, and the ticking bomb. Virginia Law Rev 91:1425–1461

Milne AJM (1972) Reason, morality and politics. In: Parekhand B, Berki RN (eds) The morality of politics, pp. 31–51

Nagel T (1978) Ruthlessness in public life. In: Hampshire S (ed) Public and private morality. Cambridge University Press, Cambridge, pp 75–91

Nozick R (1974) Anarchy, state, and utopia. Basic Books, New York

Prichard HA (1912) Does moral philosophy rest on a mistake? Mind 21:21–37

United Nations (1966) International covenant on civil and political rights. 999 UNTS 171

Urmson JO (1958) Saints and heroes. In: Melden AI (ed) Essays in moral philosophy. University of Washington Press, Seattle, pp 198–216

Walzer M (1977) Just and unjust wars: a moral argument with historical illustrations. Basic Books, New York

Walzer M (2004) Arguing about war. Yale University Press, New Haven

Wellman C (1995) Real rights. Oxford University Press, New York

Wellmn C (1997) An approach to rights. Kluwer Academic Publishers, Dordrecht

MIX
Papier aus verantwortungsvollen Quellen
Paper from responsible sources
FSC® C105338

If you have any concerns about our products,
you can contact us on
ProductSafety@springernature.com

In case Publisher is established outside the EU,
the EU authorized representative is:
Springer Nature Customer Service Center GmbH
Europaplatz 3, 69115 Heidelberg, Germany

Printed by Libri Plureos GmbH
in Hamburg, Germany